At Issue

|Violent Children

Other Books in the At Issue Series:

At Issue

Violent Children

Roman Espejo, Book Editor

GREENHAVEN PRESS
A part of Gale, Cengage Learning

GALE
CENGAGE Learning

Detroit • New York • San Francisco • New Haven, Conn • Waterville, Maine • London

Christine Nasso, *Publisher*
Elizabeth Des Chenes, *Managing Editor*

© 2010 Greenhaven Press, a part of Gale, Cengage Learning.

Gale and Greenhaven Press are registered trademarks used herein under license.

For more information, contact:
Greenhaven Press
27500 Drake Rd.
Farmington Hills, MI 48331-3535
Or you can visit our Internet site at gale.cengage.com

For product information and technology assistance, contact us at

Gale Customer Support, 1-800-877-4253
For permission to use material from this text or product, submit all requests online at www.cengage.com/permissions

Further permissions questions can be e-mailed to permissionrequest@cengage.com

Articles in Greenhaven Press anthologies are often edited for length to meet page requirements. In addition, original titles of these works are changed to clearly present the main thesis and to explicitly indicate the author's opinion. Every effort is made to ensure that Greenhaven Press accurately reflects the original intent of the authors. Every effort has been made to trace the owners of copyrighted material.

Cover image © Images.com/Corbis.

LIBRARY OF CONGRESS CATALOGING-IN-PUBLICATION DATA

Violent children / Roman Espejo, book editor.
    p. cm. -- (At issue)
    Includes bibliographical references and index.
    ISBN 978-0-7377-4446-0 (hardcover)
    ISBN 978-0-7377-4447-7 (pbk.)
    1. Youth and violence. 2. Violence in adolescence. 3. Violence in children.
    I. Espejo, Roman, 1977-
    HQ799.2.V56V57 2009
    303.60835--dc22

                                                                      2009024279

Printed in the United States of America
1 2 3 4 5 6 7 13 12 11 10 09

Contents

Introduction

In March 2009, a 15-year-old girl assaulted a 13-year-old student leaving a private-school dance in Brisbane, Australia. The victim, also a girl, had allegedly harassed the assailant's younger sister in online chat rooms, where the two sparred over their falling out and traded racial slurs. The 13-year-old sustained cuts and bruises and underwent brain scans at a hospital; the 15-year-old was suspended and faced expulsion at her school. Niall Coburn, the principal of the private school, told the *Courier-Mail*, "Unfortunately it is one of those things that begins in cyberbullying."[1]

The term "cyberbullying" is often credited to Canadian educator Bill Belsey. According to him, the act "involves the use of information and communication technologies such as e-mail, cell phone and pager text messages, instant messaging, defamatory personal Web sites, and defamatory online personal polling websites, to support deliberate, repeated, and hostile behavior by an individual or group, that is intended to harm others."[2] In addition, the National Crime Prevention Council (NCPC) declares that it has become a serious problem for American youths: "Now many teens also have lives on the Internet. And bullying has followed teens online."[3] NCPC estimates that about half of teens have been cyberbullied, which includes having undesirable digital photos posted or e-mailed without consent, being tricked into revealing personal information, and dealing with a bully pretending he or she is someone else online.

Although not directly perpetrated by her peers, the October 2006 suicide of Megan Meier, a 13-year-old from Dardenne Prairie, Missouri, brought cyberbullying to media attention. Up to the time of her death, Meier was taunted on MySpace by Lori Drew, who posed as a teenage boy on the social networking Web site to deceive and humiliate Meier after she purportedly spread rumors about Drew's daughter. As a result, a cyberbullying ordinance was enforced in Dardenne Prairie in November 2007; Drew was convicted of computer fraud more than a year later. Meier's death also sparked action to enact a national law against cyberbullying. In May 2008, Linda T. Sánchez, a California member of the U.S. House of Representatives, introduced the "Megan Meier Cyberbullying Prevention Act." (As of spring 2009, Congress had not voted on the act.)

Numerous experts believe that cyberbullying is comparable to physical teasing and badgering offline. For instance, Lisa M. Sontag, a psychology researcher at the University of Florida, maintains, "Peer victimization using the medium of cyberspace . . . carries similar negative repercussions for adolescent adjustment compared to more traditional, face-to-face forms of victimization," such as "internalizing distress."[4] Others propose that bullying online causes particular psychological and emotional harm because of the anonymity of the perpetrator, the public nature of the humiliation, and the always-on presence of the Internet. Criminal justice professors Sameer Hinduja and Justin W. Patchin state:

> There is usually an imbalance of "power" in cyberbullying situations. . . . While power in traditional bullying might be physical (stature) or social (wit or popularity), online power may simply stem from proficiency or knowledge or the possession of some content (information, pictures, or video) that can be used to inflict harm. Anyone with any of these characteristics or possessions within a certain online context has "power," which can be wielded through some form of cyberbullying.

Hinduja and Patchin continue that the World Wide Web "frees [bullies] from normative and social constraints on their behavior,"[5] heightening the maliciousness of the harassment. In the words of a 14-year-old New Jersey girl, "Being bullied . . . over the Internet is worse. It's torment and hurts."[6]

Nonetheless, critics believe that the threat and extent of cyberbullying may be exaggerated. For example, the Crimes Against Children Research Center (CCRC) concludes, "Most online harassment incidents did not appear to meet the standard definition of bullying used in school-based research and requiring aggression, repetition, and power imbalance."[7] In fact, CCRC upholds that only 9 percent of youths in the country have been cyberbullied. Furthermore, the borderless Internet may throw the reach and practicality of local cyberbullying ordinances into question. Skip Slates, a California-based computer and technology attorney, argues,

> These laws are doomed to failure. A global medium, much as the Internet, simply cannot be regulated at the local level. . . . What is legal on one side of the street may be illegal on the other side of the street in an adjacent city . . . What if the messages are composed on a laptop or cellphone while in different jurisdictions?[8]

As with graphic imagery and content in the media and entertainment, the emergence of cyberbullying reflects how the problem of violence and children may be affected by technology. In *At Issue: Violent Children*, experts, advocacy groups, policymakers, and others debate the factors that may prime youngsters for violence, examine the means that potentially facilitate such behaviors, and present possible—and often contrasting—solutions to these issues.

Notes

1. Tanya Chilcott and Robyn Ironside, *Courier-Mail*, March 31, 2009.
2. Shaheen Shariff, *Cyber-Bullying: Issues and Solutions for the School, the Classroom and the Home.* New York: Routledge, 2008.
3. NCPC, ncpc.org (Accessed April 2009).
4. Bruce K. Dixon, *Pediatric News*, June 2008.

5. A Cyberbullying Fact Sheet: What You Need to Know About Online Aggression," www.cyberbullying.us, 2009.

6. A Cyberbullying Fact Sheet: What You Need to Know About Online Aggression," www.cyberbullying.us, 2009.

7. Larry Magid, cbsnews.com, November 4, 2008.

8. Orange County Computer Lawyer Blog, December 3, 2007.

1

Youth Violence Is a Serious Problem

Kathiann M. Kowalski

Kathiann M. Kowalski is an author of children's and young adult books.

News headlines show that violent behavior among children and adolescents is a serious problem. Homicide is the second leading cause of death for youths ages 10 to 24, and a large fraction of high school students report that they recently carried a knife, gun, or other weapon, increasing the likelihood that confrontations will escalate into lethal violence. For the victims, the physical and emotional toll of violence affects them in different ways. Some young people turn to substance abuse, while others become violent themselves. Recognizing the signs and symptoms, such as a student's tendency to be verbally abusive or have anger flare-ups, is the first step in preventing youth violence.

As the headlines show, violence kills. Homicide is the second leading cause of death among young people ages 10 to 24, says the Centers for Disease Control and Prevention (CDC). In a recent survey, more than one-sixth of high school students surveyed had recently carried a knife, gun, or club.

Carrying weapons increases the risk that a fight will become fatal. Fifteen-year-old Kamal Singh was apparently try-

Kathiann M. Kowalski, "Violence Hits Hard: Violence Against Teens Can Have Devastating Consequences," *Current Health 2*, vol. 30, no. 7, March 2004, pp. 6(9). Copyright © 2004 Weekly Reader Corp. Reproduced by permission.

ing to get away from a fistfight. But instead of letting the Bronx teen run away, other teens chased Kamal and shot him.

Even if an attack isn't fatal, violence can cause serious injury. Permanent disability can change a teen's life forever. Less serious attacks cause significant pain too.

In Stafford Springs, Connecticut, parents pressed charges against a high school football star who attacked their son in the locker room. The boy needed nine stitches to stop the bleeding on his back. The football player had bullied the boy several other times too. It was time to stop the violence.

Victims' Reactions Vary

Beth was in ninth grade when Katy shoved her down some stairs. Beth fell into her friend Donna. "I felt angry—and incredulous," says Beth. Instead of hitting back, Beth helped Donna. Then she went to the high school dean. After that, Katy stayed away from Beth.

Anger and shock are typical responses to violence. But fortunately, they didn't stop Beth from handling her problem effectively. Other teens feel embarrassed or powerless. Still others want to get revenge against their attackers.

Fear is another common response. "Sometimes the fear is worse than the actual physical harm," says Lara Murray of the National Center for Victims of Crime. "Physical harm ends. Bruises heal. But that feeling of fear can last a long time— even long after the bully has gone away."

Violence is demeaning. It's a direct attack on someone's self-esteem and value as a human being. In Northbrook, Illinois, high school seniors "hazed" some juniors [in spring 2003]. Fueled by alcohol, the senior girls punched and brutalized the other students. They spread urine, feces, pig intestines, and fish guts on them. Videotape captured the event for the whole country to see.

No one wants to believe that someone they know could be so cruel. Sometimes victims deny that a problem exists. They make excuses for their attackers. Or they feel guilty themselves.

"Most often they think it's their fault—that they've done something wrong and therefore deserve it," says Robert Geffner, a psychologist in San Diego. He adds, "There is never an excuse for somebody to be abusive—verbally, emotionally, physically, or sexually. When situations like that occur, it is not the fault or the cause of the person who's being victimized."

Physical, Mental, and Emotional Pain

Violence makes victims feel uneasy and anxious. They may suffer physical symptoms such as headaches and stomachaches, or have trouble sleeping. Often they don't connect these effects with the violence they've suffered.

Students can feel too upset to concentrate on learning, and their grades may drop. Many find ways to skip school instead of going to class.

Teens who are victims of violence may experience clinical depression. They feel helpless and hopeless. They withdraw from other people. They lose interest in things they once enjoyed. Without treatment for this serious mental illness, people find it hard to function normally. In severe cases, untreated depression can lead to suicide.

Victims of violence may hurt themselves in other ways too. Many teens with eating disorders have suffered abuse. Unconsciously, they try to control one tiny portion of their lives—eating—when everything else seems out of control.

Other victims try to numb their pain. Melissa started drinking at age 9. "At that time I was experiencing sexual abuse by my father," recalls the college student, "so it was an escape from that." Rather than solving her problem, Melissa's alcohol use led to addiction. Years later, she got into recovery and got counseling for her problems.

The Cycle of Violence

Violence can make it hard for victims to form close relationships. They may not trust other people. They may be afraid of letting anyone get too close. They may never have seen healthy relationships in action.

Other victims may adopt extreme behaviors. Teens who were sexually abused sometimes become promiscuous. That makes it even harder for them to form healthy, loving relationships. It also exposes them to sexually transmitted diseases.

When violence becomes part of everyday life, teens can lose their ability to respond to other people and events on a healthy emotional level.

Victims of violence can become violent themselves. They may bottle up their anger, until one day it finally explodes. In Tununak, Alaska, three 14-year-old boys who were being bullied brought guns to school. The teens threatened to kill other students. Fortunately, police got them to surrender before they shot anyone.

Sometimes teens who grew up with domestic violence become part of a cycle of violence. They abuse other people as a way to get the upper hand and exert power over them. Other teens become victims in future relationships.

"But it's not a one-to-one relationship," stresses Geffner. "Not everyone who has been in an abusive situation or an abusive home will end up being a victim or an offender." And many people who become victims or perpetrators of violence did not grow up in violent homes. Nonetheless, an abusive family background is a risk factor, says Geffner. Counseling can help teens with such backgrounds deal with its impact.

Anxiety Takes a Toll

Sixteen-year-old Devin Fowlkes died [August 2003] when he got caught in the crossfire outside his Washington, D.C., high school. But bystanders suffer even when they don't get [hit].

School violence can make everyone uneasy. After all, you can never know who the next victim might be.

"It definitely affects the learning environment," adds Sarah Gillespie, a high school senior. "When students go to school, they need to be able to focus on their classwork and not have to worry about what's going to happen to them when they're changing classes, or what's going to happen when they go to the cafeteria or go to the bathroom."

Witnessing violence can cause emotional trauma that can bring on nightmares, flashbacks, physical illness, and general uneasiness. Frequent violence can have a numbing effect too. Teens may shrug events off and act as if nothing happened. But when violence becomes part of everyday life, teens can lose their ability to respond to other people and events on a healthy emotional level.

Violence isn't healthy for anyone. Perpetrators usually have serious psychological problems. They need help to stop their hurtful behaviors. Otherwise, they're likely to continue and escalate.

Seeing the Signs

Spotting the signs and symptoms of violence is an important first step in stopping it.

- A need to have control over someone. "One of the first warning signs is when people start trying to control somebody else," says Geffner. That can signal an unhealthy dating relationship. In a school setting, it could mark a potential bully.

- Putting people down verbally or calling them names raises another red flag.

- Intolerance of any differences is also a danger sign.

- Quick flare-ups. If someone can't handle things not going his or her way, that's a warning sign too.

If you spot these signs in any of your own relationships, watch out. Find ways to get out of the situation.

How can you help someone else who may not see the signs? If the behavior has already become physical or escalates, tell a responsible adult. "That definitely is a warning sign that somebody should be notified," says Geffner.

Otherwise, talk to the other person about what you see. Let that person know you care and are there when he or she needs you. He or she may not be ready to listen. But, says Geffner, "It's good to let the person know that there is concern, and that there are places that can help."

Taking Action

When attacks or threats occur, you need to report the offenders. That gives authorities a chance to help stop the violence— and it lessens feelings of isolation and helplessness.

When you make the decision to act, you'll feel more in control and more powerful. It's a good idea to get support from friends when making the report. Also, choose a sympathetic guidance counselor or other adult to talk to.

These actions should be taken when you or someone you know is being bullied. Bullying and hazing should never become "business as usual."

"It is important to step in and not just be bystanders," stresses Geffner, "because these things continue and escalate when nobody else says anything or supports the person who's being bullied or victimized."

"Just put yourself in the shoes of that student at the school who is constantly being bullied," urges Sarah Gillespie, a teen from Mebane, North Carolina. "The bullying and the hazing and all of that—those are forms of violence. When you think about what that student's feeling and what's going on, you realize the need to stop that violence."

2

The Problem of Youth Violence Is Exaggerated

Marilyn D. McShane and Franklin P. Williams III

Marilyn D. McShane and Franklin P. Williams III, are experts in criminal justice and editors of Youth Violence and Delinquency: Monsters and Myths, Vol. 1.

The media's dramatic, terror-filled accounts of youth violence and crime do not reflect current trends; juvenile offenders are not getting younger or committing more rapes, robberies, and murders. On the contrary, juvenile arrest rates, especially for homicide, have decreased to levels similar to the 1980s, and the vast majority of the crimes they commit are minor offenses, such as shoplifting and vandalism. In addition, schools are still very safe places, and fewer students drop out now than in the 1970s. Nonetheless, many children continue to live under the dangerous poverty limit, which increases their risk of delinquency and being victims of abuse and neglect at home.

When ancient mapmakers worked their way to the edges of unchartered or unexplored territories, they marked the boundaries with the famous phrase, "beyond here monsters lie" or "here there be dragons," appealing to the common understanding that what was unknown must contain the dreaded or evil. Much the same can be said for the vast expanse of juvenile delinquency—the wild, unpredictable, and unrestrained tempers of youth are to be feared and often demonized. The media "mapmakers" often paint dramatic and terror-filled accounts of what are, in reality, rare events. Consequently, the routine parade of countless minor episodes of kids who shoplift, run away, and vandalize, and who are overlooked in the overcrowded and overworked juvenile courts, is far less attractive for the sound bites of the evening news.

Media coverage of certain dramatic juvenile crimes tends to give people the wrong impression about current trends in delinquency.

The normal developmental tendencies of youth to talk, act, and dress in extreme and unique ways often contribute to these fearful images. The blue hair, Mohawk cuts, the cacophonic music, and elaborate piercings and tattoos often mark the borders of adult tolerance. Although generational misunderstandings and the inevitable rebellion of teenagers is nothing new, we seem to continue to approach each successive wave of youngsters with the same apprehension, fear, and readiness to suppress the wayward vestiges of individualism. So it is not surprising, then, that a crime committed by a spike-haired, nose-ringed, gothic-dressed, jackbooted young man is perhaps likely to draw more attention from the court and require longer supervision with more restrictions on activities. Anti-loitering and congregating statutes, as well as prohibitions against skateboarding, are viewed by critics as ways to cleanse business areas of unattractive nuisances. As a group of youth in Brattleboro, Vermont, gathering in downtown parking areas [and] pushing the limits of municipal goodwill found out, no law prohibited them from stripping down to various levels of nudity, but there soon would be, as fast as the select board of town leaders could legislate one.

A Distorted and Pessimistic View

Today, theorists often spend as much time contemplating why youth do not commit crime as why youth do. We attempt to explain not only the overall decrease in juvenile crime, but also why, in the face of such a decrease, most people still have the impression that the juvenile crime rate is increasing. Media coverage of certain dramatic juvenile crimes tends to give people the wrong impression about current trends in delinquency. The terms "shocking crime" and "brutal violence" are often overplayed, creating a distorted and pessimistic view of youthful offenders. Although many people believe that juvenile delinquency is increasing, the truth is that the juvenile offending rate is fairly stable and that many youth are engaged in co-offending, which tends to make the amount of crime appear higher. That is, more offenders are arrested than actual crimes committed. Also, contrary to what some people seem to believe, juvenile offenders are not getting younger or engaging in more rapes and robberies.

Although there is a great deal to be optimistic about, there is much to be done to enrich the lives of American youth.

Crime figures vary by whether you are talking about reports of crimes or arrests for crimes. As a consequence of better law enforcement techniques, arrests can increase even though the amount of reported crimes stays about the same. The accuracy of certain crime statistics and the likelihood of offenses being reported also vary by type, such as drug crime, violent crime, and status offenses, as well as by race and gender. We know that, overall, the juvenile arrest rate for property crimes has decreased. By 2003, the juvenile arrest rate for violent crime, particularly murder, had decreased to levels similar to those around the early 1980s. Some of the most recent government statistics indicate that arrests for simple assaults and aggravated assaults have increased, particularly for juvenile females. So, although there is a great deal to be optimistic about, there is much to be done to enrich the lives of American youth and to improve their chances of success.

We know that the number of children living under the poverty limit is still dangerously high and that self-reported delinquency has always been associated with being poor. As in the past, data still suggest that most juvenile crime is intraracial, thus victims are likely to be the same race as their offenders. Children continue to be at higher risk for neglect and maltreatment in the home than they are for violent victimization in the streets. Schools are still one of the safest places for kids, and fewer kids drop out today than in the 1970s.

Although data seem to indicate a rise in lethality in some crimes, the casual ease with which juveniles access semiautomatic and automatic weapons can be used to explain trends in homicide. These explanations are as insightful and as full of implications for programs and policies as those that address deviant behavior. Although narrowing our focus to specific types of offenders only or certain types of offenses may be frustrating to those seeking a "one-size-fits-all" approach, it often gives us a greater, more accurate, albeit smaller, picture. Thus, readers who are looking for clear-cut answers to the problems of juvenile crime and violence will find that there are lots of little ones, plenty of pretty good ones, and certainly none that fit a broad range of behaviors and cultures. . . . It is evident that the field requires a wide range of research from many varied disciplines and involves not only environmental, social, legal, political, and economic change but also changes in our values, attitudes, and goals—the very fabric of our society. . . .

The realities are often far less dramatic and entertaining than the news clips on evening television reporting, but they represent the true focus of law enforcement, the courts, and youth services workers in corrections, treatment, and community outreach professions. Our tax dollars, our neighbor's children, our schools, and our police are all influenced by the way we view delinquency.

3

Youth Gang Violence Is a Serious Problem

Office of Juvenile Justice and Delinquency Prevention

Office of Juvenile Justice and Delinquency Prevention (OJJDP) is part of the U.S. Department of Justice. OJJDP helps state and local governments implement effective juvenile delinquency intervention and prevention programs.

Assessing the scope of the youth gang problem is difficult, given the transitional nature of gang membership and the secrecy of their activities. Surveys show that the prevalence of gangs peaked during the mid-1990s and leveled off thereafter, decreasing in nonurban areas. However, gang activity still persists in major cities and schools nationwide. In one survey, almost eight in ten cities with populations over 50,000 report having gang problems. And gangs commit a disproportionate number of crimes, such as robberies and drug dealing. Ultimately, gang activity has lasting consequences for gang members themselves, who are at much higher risk of being victims of violence and cut off from opportunities for stability into adulthood than their peers who are not in gangs.

Accurately estimating the scope of the youth gang problem is difficult in part because of the lack of consensus about what "counts"—what combination of size, stability, hierarchy, symbolic communication, and ongoing criminal activity distinguishes a true gang from a transitory collection of indi-

Office of Juvenile Justice and Delinquency Prevention, "Chapter 3: Juvenile Offenders: The Prevalence of Youth Gangs Declined in Nonurban Areas, but Gangs Remain a Substantial Urban Problem," *Juvenile Offenders and Victims: 2006 National Report*, 2006, pp. 82–84. Reproduced by permission.

viduals, not to mention what level of involvement in and adherence to the gang distinguishes a real member from a hanger-on or "wannabe." In addition, the available sources of information on gangs are unreliable. Gangs are, after all, inherently secret groups. Outsiders are apt to miss or misinterpret signs of their presence. Insiders are liable to distort the signs.

Most Americans still live in or near areas that have problems with youth gangs.

Nevertheless, based on surveys of local authorities, it appears that the overall number of communities with active youth gangs grew sharply during the last few decades of the 20th century, peaked in the mid-1990s, and recently declined somewhat.

A comparison of the number of localities reporting problems with youth gangs during the 1970s with the number reporting gang problems in the 1990s found a tenfold increase in gang jurisdictions—including more suburban, small-town, and rural jurisdictions with reported gang problems than ever before. On the basis of law enforcement agency responses to the 1996 National Youth Gang Survey, which gathered data on gangs from a representative sample of police and sheriff departments across the country, the nation's total youth gang membership was estimated at more than 846,000, with 31,000 gangs operating in 4,824 local jurisdictions. Estimates based on subsequent surveys have steadily receded from those highs. Based on [a] 2004 survey, youth gang membership was estimated at 760,000 and total youth gangs at 24,000. Youth gangs were estimated to be active in more than 2,900 jurisdictions served by city (population of 2,500 or more) and county law enforcement agencies.

The drop between 1996 and 2004 in the number of localities reporting gang problems was almost entirely attributable to small cities and suburban and rural jurisdictions—where gang problems had tended to be relatively minor and less persistent. Nearly 8 in 10 cities with populations of 50,000 or more continued to report gang problems. Thus, most Americans still live in or near areas that have problems with youth gangs.

A Third of Public School Principals Report Gang Activity in Their Schools

In a 1999–2000 survey of a nationally representative sample of public school principals, 18% reported "undesirable gang activities" in their schools—including 31% of the middle school and 37% of the secondary school principals. Apart from being more common in schools located in urban areas, in poor communities, and in communities with large minority populations, gang activity was strongly linked with school size: principals of schools with enrollments of 1,000 or more were about 4 times more likely to report gang activity than those with enrollments of less than 500.

In 2001 and again in 2003, as part of the School Crime Supplement to the National Crime Victimization Survey, students ages 12–18 were asked about the presence of gangs in their schools during the prior 6 months. In both years, about 1 in 5 reported that gangs were present. Among minority students, students in city schools, and those in upper grades, much higher proportions reported gang presence. For instance, in 2003, 42% of urban Hispanic students said they attended schools in which gangs were present.

Youth Gang Members Are Overwhelmingly Male and Predominantly Minorities

Law enforcement agencies responding to National Youth Gang Surveys over a number of years have reported demographic details regarding gang members in their jurisdictions, including age, gender, and racial and ethnic background. Although reported characteristics varied considerably by locality—with emergent gangs in less populous areas tending to have more white and more female members—overall, gang demographics have been fairly consistent from year to year.

Estimated race/ethnicity of U.S. youth gang members, 2004:

Hispanic	49%
Black	37
White	8
Asian	5
Other	1
Total	100%

On the basis of responses to the 2004 survey, gang membership was estimated to be 94% male. Youth gang membership was estimated to consist of 41% juveniles and 59% young adults (18 or older).

Gang demographic profiles based on law enforcement estimates differ from profiles emerging from youth surveys. Self-reported gang members tend to include many more females and nonminority males. For example, in one large-scale 1995 survey of public school 8th graders, 25% of self-reported gang members were white and 38% were female. Even when more restrictive criteria for gang membership were applied to these self-report results—in an effort to filter out fringe or inactive members and isolate only the most active core gang members—significant demographic differences from law enforcement estimates persisted.

Law enforcement estimates of nationwide juvenile gang membership suggest that no more than about 1% of all youth ages 10–17 are gang members. Self-reports, such as the 1997 National Longitudinal Survey of Youth (NLSY97), find that 2% of youth ages 12–17 (3% of males and 1% of females) say they were in a gang in the past year. NLSY97 also found that 8% of 17-year-olds (11% of males and 6% of females) said they had ever belonged to a gang. These proportions obviously vary considerably from place to place. For example, researchers tracking a sample of high-risk youth in Rochester, NY, reported that 30% joined gangs between the ages of 14 and 18.

Gang membership tends to be short-lived, even among high-risk youth. Among the Rochester gang members, half of the males and two-thirds of the females stayed in gangs for a year or less, with very few youth remaining gang members throughout their adolescent years.

Many Factors Are Related to Whether Youth Join Gangs

When asked directly what led them to join gangs, 54% of Rochester gang members said they had followed the lead of friends or family members who preceded them, 19% said they did it for protection, and 15% said it was for fun or excitement. Younger gang members were somewhat more likely to cite protection as the primary motivation.

However they may characterize their own motivations, gang members' backgrounds commonly include certain features that may make them more inclined to join gangs. The following risk factors have been found to predict gang membership:

- Individual factors: early delinquency (especially violence and drug use) and early dating and precocious sexual activity.

- Family factors: non-two-parent structure, poverty, and other gang-involved members.

- School factors: low achievement, commitment, and aspirations; truancy; negative labeling by teachers; and lack of a sense of safety in school.

- Peer factors: associations with delinquent or aggressive peers.

- Community factors: poverty, drug availability, gang presence, lack of a sense of safety and attachment.

[Seattle] gang members were 3 times more likely to say they had been arrested, and 5 times more likely to say they had sold drugs.

Some risk factors are more predictive than others. In a longitudinal study of youth living in high-crime neighborhoods in Seattle, for example, pre-adolescents (ages 10–12) who later joined gangs were distinguished most markedly by very early marijuana use, neighborhood conditions making marijuana readily available, and learning disabilities. The presence of any of these factors in a juvenile's background more than tripled the odds of his or her later becoming a gang member. Childhood risk factors that were predictive of later sustained (as opposed to transient) gang membership included early violence, acting out, and association with antisocial peers.

The more risk factors present in a youth's background, the more likely that youth is to join a gang. In Seattle, for example, those with two or three identified risk factors at ages 10–12 were 3 times more likely to go on to join a gang than those with none or one, those with four to six risk factors were 5 times more likely, and those with seven or more were 13 times more likely. Having background risk factors in more than one area of life—that is, individual, family, community, etc.—increases the likelihood of gang involvement even more than a general accumulation of factors. The Rochester study, which divided risk factors into seven general domains, found that 61% of the boys and 40% of the girls with problems in all seven areas were gang members.

Gang Members Are Responsible for a Disproportionate Share of Offenses

By their own account, gang members are more likely to engage in criminal activity than their peers. In response to interview questions regarding their activities in the prior month, Seattle gang members were 3 times more likely than nongang members to report committing break-ins and assaults, 4 times more likely to report committing felony thefts, and 8 times more likely to report committing robberies. When asked about their activities during the prior year, gang members were 3 times more likely to say they had been arrested, and 5 times more likely to say they had sold drugs.

In surveys of high-risk youth, gang members represent a minority of these youth but account for most of the reported crime. In the Rochester study, gang members made up 30% of the sample but accounted for 54% of the arrests, 68% of the property crimes, 69% of the violent offenses, 70% of the drug sales, and 82% of the serious delinquencies. A similar study of high-risk Denver youth found that gang members constituted just 14% of the sample but committed 80% of the serious and violent crimes.

Guns Are a Key Factor in Gang Members' Heightened Criminality

A body of longitudinal research discredits the notion that gangs are simply collections of antisocial individuals who would be offending at the same rates even if they were not organized into gangs. For one thing, gang members have been found to be more criminally active and violent than delinquents who are not gang affiliated, even those who associate to the same extent with other delinquents. Furthermore, this heightened criminality and violence occur only during periods of gang membership—not before or after. Rochester juveniles who were gang members during only 1 year between ages 14 and 18 committed more offenses during that 1 gang year than they did in any of the remaining 3 years. Denver youth involved in gangs over some part of a 5-year period committed 85% of their serious violent offenses, 86% of their serious property offenses, and 80% of their drug sales while gang-involved. All of these findings strongly suggest that the gang structure itself tends to facilitate or even demand increased involvement in delinquency.

Young adults who had been in gangs were more likely to have ended their education prematurely . . . and failed to establish stable work lives.

A significant factor may be the strong association between gang membership and gun possession. Gang members are far more likely than nonmembers to own or have access to guns, to carry them on the street, and to use them to commit crimes. Gang membership both facilitates juveniles' access to guns—through illegal markets and through borrowing—and provides strong and constant incentives for being armed in public. Rochester gang members' rates of gun-carrying were 10 times higher than those of nonmembers. For these youth, gun-carrying not only multiplies opportunities to commit violent crimes and raises the risk that ordinary disputes will escalate into violence—it may increase a youth's crime-readiness by supplying an all-purpose, aggressive confidence that unarmed youth do not have.

Gang Membership Has Lasting Negative Consequences

Being a member of a gang sharply raises a young person's risk of being a *victim* of violence, not just a perpetrator. Gangs may harm members in subtle as well as obvious ways, cutting them off from people and opportunities that could help them with the transition to adulthood and disrupting their lives even after they have moved beyond the gang.

Researchers tracking the lives of Rochester gang members to age 22 found evidence of serious adult dysfunction that could not be explained by other factors. Young adults who had been in gangs were more likely to have ended their education prematurely, become pregnant or had children early, and failed to establish stable work lives—all of which were associated with an increased likelihood of being arrested as adults. The differences were more notable among those who had been in gangs for a long time and persisted even when gang members were compared with nonmembers who had histories of delinquency and association with delinquent peers.

4

The Youth Gang Violence Problem Is Exaggerated

Justice Policy Institute

Based in Washington, D.C., the Justice Policy Institute (JPI) is a criminal justice think tank that promotes alternatives to incarceration.

The media and numerous lawmakers assert that gang-related violence and activity is a "national crisis" threatening everyone. But crime has been in decline over the last decade in the United States, particularly offenses perpetrated by youth gangs. According to a Federal Bureau of Investigation (FBI) report, arguments accounted for four times as many homicides than gang activity. Furthermore, between 1994 and 2003, the rate of reported violent victimizations by perceived gang members fell 73 percent. The profiles of gang members and their victims are also distorted. In contrast to assumptions, the majority of gang members outgrow delinquency with guidance and support, and gang violence affects minorities far more than whites.

Although crime has been decreasing in the United States for [more than a decade] many people fear that violent crime, especially gang-related crime, is rising. While no one disputes the need to effectively respond to violent crime that disproportionately affects certain communities and neighborhoods, questions remain on the pervasiveness of gang crime and the nature of appropriate responses. Currently, public opinion is swayed by sensationalized stories from media and

Justice Policy Institute, "A Policy Brief, Ganging Up on Communities? Putting Gang Crime in Context," 2005. Reproduced by permission.

lawmakers who say that gang-related crime is a "national crisis," requiring new federal and state legislation, mandatory minimums, and new powers to arrest, detain, imprison, and deport young people.

Expensive and Ineffective Responses to Crime

In 2005, several new pieces of federal legislation are being advanced to address the "gang crisis," federalizing law enforcement efforts that have historically been the jurisdiction of the states. The "Gang Prevention and Effective Deterrence Act of 2005" is winding its way through the Senate, and would create new gang offenses, enhance existing penalties, lower the number of people defined as a gang from five to three, and transfer more youth to adult courts and prisons. The Senate bill comes after the passage of a House bill, the "Gang Deterrence and Community Protection Act of 2005," which calls for new mandatory minimums for gang-related offenses, and an expansion of the death penalty. [Editor's note: The bill did not become law.]

The reach of the gang crisis is portrayed as broad and omnipresent, said to connect to everything from drug trafficking, to immigration, to terrorism. In June [2005], Representative J. Randy Forbes introduced the "Alien Gang Removal Act [the bill did not become law]," a bill that authorizes the Department of Homeland Security (DHS) to deport groups, and associations that are designated as "criminal street gangs."

These bills were introduced to reduce gang crime, yet they rely almost exclusively on approaches that have been shown to be the most expensive and least effective ways to respond to crime. Responding to provisions to transfer youth to adult prison, Robert Shepherd, Professor of Law at the University of Richmond and former Virginia prosecutor, says: "this bill flies in the face of what works with young people . . . the evidence shows that trying young people as adults exacerbates rather than lessens crime." Shepherd suggests that "rather than federalizing crime with policies that will not solve the problem, we should provide federal resources and support for state intervention and prevention programs."

In testimony before House Committee on the Judiciary, David Cole, Professor of Law at Georgetown University Law School, said that [the "Alien Gang Removal Act"] "will empower the DHS to deport foreign nationals who have never committed any crimes whatsoever, and who have obeyed all of our laws, simply because the DHS has determined that they are members of designated street gangs." . . .

According to Leading National Indicators, Crime and Gang Crimes are Falling

To understand the magnitude, nature and impact [of] crime in the nation, experts and scholars rely largely on two statistical programs administered by the U.S. Department of Justice: the Uniform Crime Reporting (UCR) Program and the National Crime Victimization Survey (NCVS). While these are two different reporting devices that rely on two different methodologies to count crime, together, they provide a picture of the nation's crime problem.

In Chicago, reported to be a site of "super gangs," there was a 35% decrease in the reported number of violent crimes in between mid-year 1999 and 2004.

The UCR data is compiled from monthly law enforcement reports or individual crime incident records transmitted directly to the FBI or to centralized state agencies that then report to the FBI. In 2003, law enforcement agencies representing approximately 291 million U.S. inhabitants reported to the UCR Program, which is the equivalent to 93% of the total population.

Despite fears of proliferating gang violence in recent years, violent crime throughout the U.S. has steadily decreased. According to the latest crime survey under the FBI's UCR program, the number of violent crimes decreased 1.7% between 2003 and 2004. According to the FBI's Supplemental Homicide Report, in 2002, four times as many homicides were related to an argument than were related to gang activity.

Several provisions of the ["Gang Prevention and Effective Deterrence Act of 2005"] and similar legislation that passed the House specifically call for new federal powers to prosecute 16- and 17-year-old youth as adults for gang crimes, including homicide. But according to the FBI Uniform Crime Reports, the number of people nationwide reported to be arrested in 2003 for either a "gangland" or "juvenile gang homicide" is small, totaling 1,111—approximately 7% of the 16,503 homicide arrests that year. Of those, only 111 were reported to be under 18 years of age.

According to the most recent UCR, serious violent crime is also on the decline in the cities most identified with a gang problem. In Chicago, reported to be a site of "super gangs," there was a 35% decrease in the reported number of violent crimes in between mid-year 1999 and 2004. The most recent reporting period (mid-year 2003–4) saw homicide arrests fall by 25%, and robbery arrests fall by 8%.

In Los Angeles, where gang crime has been reported to be severe, there was a 9% drop in violent crime reported between mid-year 1999 and 2004. The most recent reporting period (mid-year 2003–4) saw no change in homicide arrests, and 12% decline in violent crime. One University of Southern California study showed that gang homicides have significantly decreased between 1992 and 1998 in Los Angeles, during a time when crime generally declined in Los Angeles, California, and the United States. Whereas gang-related homicides in Los Angeles fell by 50% over this period, overall reported homicides in the city fell by 61%, and California saw a 45%

decline in reported homicides. This suggests that gang crime trends track overall crime trends, or, put another way, when crime is falling, gang crimes are likely to be falling as well.

Reports and Indicators of Gang Violence

The Bureau of Justice Statistics' (BJS) National Crime Victimization Survey (NCVS) provides another picture of crime incidents, victims, and trends. Two times a year, U.S. Census Bureau interviews a nationally representative sample of approximately 42,000 households (about 75,000 people), in which respondents are asked about crimes suffered by individuals and households and whether or not those crimes were reported to law enforcement. The NCVS estimates and extrapolates their survey findings to the rest of the nation.

The most recent BJS analysis of the NCVS, "Violence by Gang Members, 1993–2003," echoes the findings of the UCR, reporting that gang violence, like most violent crime, peaked in the early 1990s. Since the 1990s, however, "violence by perceived gang members declined over most of the 11-year period." Between 1994 and 2003, the NCVS shows that the rate of reported violent victimizations by perceived gang members fell from 5.2 per 1,000 to 1.4 per 1,000—a decline of 73%. BJS reports, *"violent crimes for which victims identified the offender to be a gang member peaked in 1996 at 10% of all violent crime and decreased until 1998 to about 6%, not significantly changing since."*

According to the BJS analysis of the NCVS, police were as likely to be notified when the victims believed the offender *not* to be a gang member (45% of violence reported to the police) as when they believed the offender belonged to a gang (47% reported). This suggests that, whether or not a victim perceived a crime to be a gang crime had little effect on whether they reported the crime to the police. In other words, for this national crime measure, the reporting of gang crimes are not necessarily underreported just because the victim perceived the assailant to be in a gang.

The national leading crime indicators suggest that gang crime is not something that happens everywhere. Concern for gang-related violence, historically and recently, has been concentrated in Los Angeles, Chicago, and other big cities. But even in these cities, gangs are concentrated in certain areas, and crime does not impact everyone equally. The gangs are centralized in neighborhoods within the city, specifically those areas that are struggling economically.

A researcher studying the reemergence of gangs in Milwaukee found that their resurgence was due to the process of deindustrialization, and consequently, the lack of entry level manufacturing jobs available to previous gang members who matured out of gang-related activity.

While African American young males face some challenges "aging out" of [gang] behavior before adulthood . . . they are just as likely to mature out of delinquent behavior as white men are.

According to one Los Angeles study published in the *Journal of Trauma: Injury, Infection and Critical Care* that analyzed the correlation between gang-related homicide at the community level and eight socioeconomic factors, the strongest correlations with gang violence were employment and income. In communities where unemployment rates were between 14% and 16%, there were 15 times as many gang homicides as neighborhoods where the unemployment rate was 4% to 7%. As the study concludes, "the community-level correlations between unemployment, lower income and gang-related homicides suggest that community-based economic programs may be more effective than conventional criminal justice suppression and education reform programs."

Given the Right Support, Most Youth "Age Out" of Delinquent Behavior

While gang membership does not automatically equal criminality, research has shown that adolescents who join street gangs are more involved in delinquent behavior than are adolescents who are not involved in gangs, and this has been shown to be true for serious and violent offenders. Even as the media, policymakers, and law enforcement promote the idea that much of the violent behavior of young men is solely gang-induced, evidence shows that some of these acts can instead be attributed to youth behavior caused by other factors. According to a report to Congress on juvenile violence research from the Office of Juvenile Justice and Delinquency Prevention (OJJDP), individual factors contribute to a male juvenile's involvement in violent behavior: Studies show that all males around the age of 15 are more likely to engage in serious delinquency, whether they belong to a gang or not. According to a report of the Surgeon General on youth violence that summarizes research from the Monitoring the Future survey, in 1998 about 30% of high school seniors reported engaging in behavior that qualifies to be measured under their "violent index": self-reported behavior that includes "hitting an instructor or supervisor, getting in a serious fight at school or work, taking part in a fight where a group of your friends were against another group, [or] hurt[ing] somebody bad enough to need a doctor." This rate of this behavior has been relatively stable for almost 20 years, in sharp contrast to the dramatic increase in youth arrests—suggesting that we may be using a justice system response for behavior that has occurred for sometime.

[According to] Dr. Delbert Elliott, Director of the Center for the Study and Prevention of Violence (CSPV), at the University of Colorado, employment is central to "maturing out" of delinquent behavior. His research shows that, while African American young males face some challenges "aging out" of this behavior before adulthood, when they have a steady job, or a significant social bond, such [as] a mentor, or a spouse, they are just as likely to mature out of delinquent behavior as white men are. Elliott's research suggests that [to] address other factors, like employment, would [be] effective at reducing crime.

So, delinquency happens often—more often than indicated by the number of youth who are arrested (who are disproportionately non-white)—suggesting that our response to youth crime doesn't necessarily impact different races and ethnicities in the same way. While a third of youth may engage in serious delinquency, researchers from the Pre-trial Resource Center reported that 82% of youth charged in select adult courts were minority youth, and that 7 out of 10 youth sentenced to an adult correctional term were African American or Latino. Whether they are in a gang or not, African Americans and Latinos disproportionately bare the brunt of policies designed to incarcerate young people in the juvenile justice and adult system.

African American and Latino Youth are More Likely to be Impacted by Gang Crime

Despite popular assumptions that gang crime impacts everyone, everywhere equally, victims of gang crimes are disproportionately non-white. While the majority of Americans are white, the National Crime Victimization Survey finds that African Americans are 1.5 times more likely to report being a victim of gang violence than whites. The NCVS also shows that Hispanics are more than *twice* as likely to be a victim of gang violence. This suggests that what is true about crime generally is true about gang crime: the people and communities most likely to be impacted by unacceptable levels of crime are African American or Hispanic, who also now comprise nearly two-thirds of the people incarcerated in the United States. So, whether policymakers choose employment and income support, or criminal justice responses to alleviate gang crime, non-white communities are more likely to be impacted [by] these policy choices.

5

Media Violence Causes Youth Violence

American Academy of Family Physicians

The American Academy of Family Physicians (AAFP) is a medical specialty society that represents more than 90,000 family physicians.

Media violence is pervasive in the lives of American children and adolescents, and its link to actual violence is supported by a massive body of literature. Media images of violent acts frequently fail to associate such behavior with pain, remorse, and long-term consequences, desensitizing youths and skewing their expectations of actual violence. Additionally, studies have shown that media violence increases aggression and leads to feelings of fear and victimization. Efforts should be made to limit and monitor youths' exposure to violent media. Media literacy programs can also help young viewers to understand the differences between actual and fictionalized violence.

Public outcry followed the 1999 shooting in a Littleton, Colorado, school that left 15 students dead and 23 injured. In truth, however, homicides that occur at school, or on the way to and from school, represent only 1 percent of total homicides among youth aged 5–19.

One can begin to appreciate the true toll of violence in the United States when comparing it with violence in other industrialized nations. In 1998, for instance, the United States experienced 35 times as many gun deaths per capita as England

and 285 times as many as Japan. Overall, a US child is about 300 times as likely to die from a firearm as a child from a typical industrialized nation.

Among Americans aged 15–34 years, two of the top three causes of death are homicide and suicide. In a given year, more US children will die from gunfire than will die from cancer, pneumonia, influenza, asthma, and HIV/AIDS combined. Other forms of violence, such as beating, stabbing, and rape also contribute significantly to US morbidity and mortality.

Media Violence in the United States

Violence is ubiquitous in American mass media. An average American youth will witness 200,000 violent episodes on television alone before age 18. Violence is often considerable, even in programs which are not advertised as violent. Overall, weapons appear on prime time television an average of 9 times each hour. An estimated 54 percent of American children can watch this programming from the privacy of their own bedrooms.

Children's shows are particularly violent. Saturday morning cartoons contain 20–25 violent acts per hour, about 6 times as many as prime time programs. Overall, 46 percent of TV violence occurs in cartoons. Additionally, these programs are more likely to juxtapose violence with humor (67 percent) and less likely to show the long-term consequences of violence (5 percent). Although some claim that cartoon violence is not as "real" and therefore not as damaging, cartoon violence has been shown to increase the likelihood of aggressive, antisocial behavior in youth. This makes sense in light of children's developmental difficulty discerning the real from the fantastic.

Media violence presents a picture significantly different from that of true violence. First, the sheer volume of violence is exaggerated; 66 percent of television programs contain violence. More significant, however, are the skewed contexts in which media present violence. In media portrayals, 75 percent of violent acts are committed without remorse, criticism, or penalty; 41 percent are associated with humor; 38 percent are committed by attractive perpetrators; and 58 percent involve victims who show no pain.

In one study, portrayals of violence against women in sexual contexts fostered callous attitudes toward victims of sexual and spousal abuse.

A Skewed Sense of Violence

This inappropriate presentation of violence leads to inappropriate expectations of youth with regard to true violence. In particular, three major attitudes are learned: aggression, desensitization, and victimization. Statistical analyses show what type of media violence most likely teaches each attribute: violent episodes associated with humor, weapons, and attractive perpetrators increase real-life aggression; humor-associated violence and graphic violence lead to real-life desensitization; and graphic violence and realistic violence tend to generate fear and a sense of victimization in viewers.

Aggression. That media violence leads to increased actual violence has been borne out by a massive body of literature. More than 1,000 lab experiments, cross-sectional analyses, longitudinal studies, and epidemiologic studies support this hypothesis, as do meta-analyses.

Many of these studies have additionally shown that certain populations are particularly sensitive to media violence. These include males, emotionally labile children, delinquent children, and children with developmental disabilities.

Desensitization. Media violence has also been shown to desensitize humans to violence. In one study, portrayals of violence against women in sexual contexts fostered callous attitudes toward victims of sexual and spousal abuse. Subjects viewed "slasher" films and were then asked, in a seemingly un-related study, to observe and comment on a videotaped rape trial. After repeated viewing of the "slasher" films, subjects showed less sympathy toward victims of rape, perceived less violence in the films, perceived films as less violent toward women, and showed decreases in anxiety and depression due to the rape trial.

Trauma and Victimization. Media violence also leads to fear and a feeling of victimization. In one study, 75 percent of high school students reported media violence at moderate to high levels, and 10 percent sought counseling due to night-mares, anxiety, and fear associated with media violence. An-other study of 3rd to 8th graders confirmed the relationship between trauma symptoms (such as nightmares) and increased television viewing.

After the [terrorist attacks] of September 11, 2001, many Americans developed symptoms of post-traumatic stress dis-order (PTSD). One study determined that increased television viewing for the few days after the event was a stronger predic-tor of PTSD than living in New York City, having had a friend or relative involved in the event, or even having actually been inside the World Trade Center that day.

The Cost of Media Violence in the United States and Worldwide

In spite of the wealth of data connecting media and actual violence, the extent of damage on our society remains in question. One researcher explored epidemiologically the intro-duction of television into various societies. He found that the homicide rate consistently doubled in different societies (United States, Canada, and South Africa) during the 10–15 year period after the introduction of television, whenever that happened to be. He extrapolated that, had TV never been in-troduced, each year the United States would have 10,000 fewer homicides, 70,000 fewer rapes, and 700,000 fewer injurious as-saults.

With American media quickly spreading across the world, the problem has become global. Researchers believe that, as of 1993, media violence was responsible for about 5–15 percent of total actual world violence.

Educational efforts should be developed to help children understand the divide between real and fictionalized violence.

Although most research on media violence has involved television and film, other types of media violence likely contribute to societal violence as well. Violent video games have been shown to increase aggression and delinquency. The two youths responsible for the killings in Littleton, CO, avidly played *Doom*, a violent video game used to train soldiers to kill. They created a customized version of the game involving two shooters with unlimited ammunition, extra weapons, and defenseless victims—a fantasy which they later brought to reality in their high school. More research needs to be done on the potential of computerized video games, the Internet, and other media to increase violence.

Future Directions

Limiting exposure is one method of lessening the impact of violent media on youth. This can be achieved informally or through the use of technology which "locks out" certain channels or amounts of television. This does not, however, affect the amount of film violence or other types of media violence consumed. Although film ratings and advisory labels can help parents decide on programs to be avoided, there are two major problems with relying on this system. First, certain labels, such as "parental discretion advised" and "R" have been shown to attract children, especially boys. Second, as has been noted, violence is present in many programs not considered to be violent, such as children's cartoons.

In addition to limiting exposure to violent media, educational efforts should be developed to help children understand the divide between real and fictionalized violence. Such media literacy programs have been shown to be effective, both in limiting the negative effects of media as well as in exploring the potential positive and pro-social uses of media.

In summary, the following measures are recommended:

1. Physicians should become involved in media education by

   - learning about the potential health risks of media consumption;

   - questioning patients about excessive exposure to media violence;

   - incorporating warnings about the health risks of violent media consumption into their preventative services; and

   - limiting video and television use in waiting rooms and substituting educational materials.

2. Families should limit and monitor media consumption.

   - Children under 2 years of age should be discouraged from watching television. Before this age, direct social interaction is critical to brain development, and television has been shown to interfere with such interaction.

   - Other children and adults should limit media consumption to less than an average of 1–2 hours a day.

   - Adults should monitor the various media to which their children are exposed, including TV, films, video games, music videos, and the Internet.

3. Policy changes should accompany our newfound understanding of the impact of media violence on public health.

   • Federal, state, and local restrictions on media violence should be increased.

   • Physicians and community members should partner with media producers to limit the amount and type of violence produced.

4. Media education and media literacy programs should be encouraged.

   • Whenever possible, adults should watch with their children and help them process media violence. Taping programs beforehand enables pausing for discussion or processing.

   • Media education programs that focus on demystifying and processing media violence should be developed and implemented. Emphasis should be placed on the inappropriate, unrealistic nature of violence on television and in films, and the consequences, responsibility, and complexity involved with true violence.

6

The Negative Effects
of Media Violence Have
Not Been Established

David Trend

David Trend is the author of The Myth of Media Violence: A
Critical Introduction *and a professor of studio art at the University of California, Irvine.*

*The debate surrounding media violence and its alleged effects
has not come to a resolution. One major problem is the difficulty
in defining media violence itself: Representations of violence are
deeply ingrained in culture and appear in storytelling, mythology, literature, art, recorded history, and the news. Also, not all
portrayals of violence are alike or produce the same reaction,
which further complicates the debate. And the competing views
of consumers, experts, politicians, and other groups are often
rhetorical and play on the fears of the public. Consequently,
voices that combine perspectives from different areas—social science, film and cultural studies, politics, and economics—are
lacking in the media violence discussion.*

The media violence question has resisted resolution in part
because the topic is so hard to define. At first, most people
have no trouble calling to mind a violent image from a cop
show, horror movie, or video game. But is media violence
simply a matter of depicting physical harm? Does it need to
be aggressive or intentional? What about accidents or natural

David Trend, "Introduction: What Is Media Violence? The Cacophony of Voices," *The
Myth of Media Violence: A Critical Introduction*, Indianapolis, IN: Wiley-Blackwell, 2007.
Reproduced by permission.

disasters? Does psychological torment count? What about verbal or implied violence? Are there degrees of violence? Is justified violence better for viewers than the gratuitous variety? What about humorous violence? Sports? How about violent documentaries? Or the nightly news?

Some of the more alarmist voices in the media violence field have claimed a young person will witness 200,000 simulated violent acts and 16,000 dramatized murders by the age of 18.

Part of the problem is that violent representations are so deeply ingrained in our culture. For centuries violence has been an important element of storytelling, and violent themes appear in the classical mythology of many nations, masterpieces of literature and art, folklore and fairy tales, opera, and theater. Religious texts like the Bible and the Koran use episodes of violence to dramatize moral lessons and to teach people to care for each other. Fairy tales warn children about the violent consequences of not behaving as instructed by adults. Great paintings and public monuments record human history with depictions of violence. And what about violence today? Eliminating violence from home entertainment has become a lot more feasible now that TVs are built with V-Chips. But what would that mean? Getting rid of offerings like *Fear Factor* and *The Amityville Horror* (2005) on the basis of violence alone would also rule out important films like *Saving Private Ryan* (1998), *Schindler's List* (1993), or *Hotel Rwanda* (2004)—not to mention popular children's films from *The Lion King* (1994) to *The Shaggy Dog* (2006).

The ubiquity of violent representations has made them a part of everyday life, and their volume keeps growing. Pick up any newspaper or turn on the TV and you will find either violent imagery or a story about violent media. Like the war on poverty, the war on drugs, and the war on terrorism, campaigns to stem the tide of media violence have failed. The most systematic quantitative studies of media violence are those conducted about television, where the frequency of violent incidents can be assessed relative to total programming. Some of the more alarmist voices in the media violence field have claimed a young person will witness 200,000 simulated violent acts and 16,000 dramatized murders by the age of 18.

The Value of Violence Depends on Its Context

Researchers studying media violence have attempted to arrive at "scientific" definitions in efforts to measure media violence. In the 1960s and 1970s this often meant something as simple as counting the number of times a character threw a punch or shot a gun, with incidents on *Colombo*, *Star Trek*, and *Get Smart* all given the same weight. No distinctions were drawn between realism, fantasy, and comedy until the 1980s, when some researchers began considering the plausibility or effects of violent incidents, as well as psychological aggression. Efforts to define media violence reached a watershed moment in the mid-1990s, when a consortium of research universities conducted the National Television Violence Study (NTVS), analyzing over 10,000 hours of broadcast material. Studying 23 channels, the NTVS found 18,000 violent acts for each week of programs it analyzed—or 6.5 incidents per channel per hour. The study determined that the average adult watched four hours of television each day. Children watched three hours a day. These patterns persist. Violence is seen on TV by people of all ages. In addition to the violence regularly seen in television dramas, sports, and Saturday morning cartoons, news coverage of war, terrorism, and crime has increased the sense of immediacy and realism in televisual violence. This has been amplified by the rise of reality-based programs and the generalized message that the world is becoming a more dangerous place.

The NTVS was the first study of its size to argue the importance of context in considering violent material, making the startling statement that "not all portrayals of violence are the same." It makes a difference, the NTVS stated, whether the violence is presented graphically on-screen or simply implied. It matters what type of character commits the violence, why, and with what kind of consequence. Is the violence committed by a hero or "good guy"? Is the action justified or rewarded? Does the violence cause pain and suffering? Or perhaps it seems to have no effect at all, as in many cartoons and comedy programs. Do we sympathize with the victim? Or not? Finally, who is the audience for the violence? The NTVS argued forcefully that not all people react to violence in the same way. The point is that not all media violence is created equal. But rarely are these many distinctions and nuances mentioned in public debates over these issues.

The Demand for Movies and Video Games

The potency of violent depictions in movies is continually enhanced by computer-generated special effects. This not only makes for more spectacular pyrotechnics[, i]t also has blurred the line between reality and fantasy as never before. The incidence of gore may not have increased over that brought to movies by the "new violence" directors of the 1990s like Abel Ferrara, Oliver Stone, and Quentin Tarantino, but the formal means by which violence could be visualized and thus imagined grew with advances in technology. Science fiction films like *Revenge of the Sith* (2005) and *X-Men: The Last Stand* (2006) introduce new kinds of blasters, phasers, and aliens as horror films like *Saw III* (2006), *Slither* (2006), and *Ghost Rider* (2007) suggest that vampires and other killers can materialize just about anytime from thin air. A spate of war films like *Troy* (2004), *Flyboys* (2006), and *Pathfinder* (2006) use digital technology to bring thousands of combatants to the screen, as have fantasy movies like the *Lord of the Rings* trilogy

(2000–4). Popular imports like *Ichi the Killer* (2002), *The Grudge 2* (2006), and *Tsotsi* (2006) have vividly portrayed mass murder and suicide—often focusing on teenage victims—as computer effects have allowed martial-arts films like *Hero* (2004), *House of Flying Daggers* (2005), and *Fearless* (2006) to launch physical combat into supernatural dimensions. Some analysts assert that the aesthetics of media violence simply satisfies existing audience desires for violent fare. In the 1960s, anthropologist Karl Lorenz argued that primitive instincts in people make them seek out stimulating experiences. [Academic] George Gerbner has concluded in what he terms "cultivation theory" that viewers become acclimated to ever more potent forms of violent representation that raise their thresholds for such material and heighten the level of intensity of programs they seek. [Academic] Dolf Zillmann has made similar assertions in articles and research papers. It's worth noting in this context that some researchers have argued that media violence is less appealing to audiences than TV formats like comedy or game shows.

Computer games are fast advancing to become the leading source of violent entertainment as market penetration in 2005 surpassed 50 percent of the US population. In 2002, people around the world spent $31 billion on computer games versus $14 billion on movies. The Entertainment Software Association asserts that adult game players (39 percent of whom are women) spend 7.5 hours per week engaged in the activity and that 84 percent of people playing computer games are over the age of 18. Some in the media violence community believe that the interactive character of computer games makes them a more influential "teacher" of aggressive behavior than movies or television, although such assertions have yet to be proven conclusively by scientific research. Regardless of its effects, computer gaming has become an enormous business—with the budgets of game development and promotion now surpassing that of many feature films. This is hardly surprising in light of the fact that popular games like *Grand Theft Auto: San Andreas* (2004) and *Halo 2* (2004) both sold over 2.4 million copies (retailing at $49.95) on their first day of release, putting them on an economic par with the most successful Hollywood movies. With 957,000 units sold, the number one game of 2005 was *World of Warcraft*, which placed participants in an environment where they hunted, shot, and blasted hundreds of other players.

It matters what type of character commits the violence, why, and with what kind of consequence.

A Cacophony of Voices

Further complicating the media violence debate are the vast differences among the participants—and their varied ways of thinking and talking about this complex issue. Parents may approach media violence quite differently from professors who study the subject or the industry professionals who produce it. Then factor in variances in parents' religious beliefs and level of education, the professors' academic discipline and definition of "truth," and the industry professionals' medium and intended audience. At best this is a recipe for misunderstanding and frustration. In the highly charged and often emotionally laden discourse of media violence it also has been a formula for distortion and dishonesty.

Put another way, debates over media violence can be viewed as symptoms of larger concerns over social values, behaviors, and the role communications technologies play in people's lives. Because media violence has prompted concern among such a vast and diverse set of groups, it has generated a fragmented array of questions, accusations, hypotheses, and answers, many of which address important aspects of the media violence debate, but few that adequately consider its complexities, interrelationships, and contradictions.

One can identify perspectives in this fragmented media discussion from six groups, each with its own agenda and ways of talking about the issue. Given their varying reasons for looking at media violence and the different ways they perceive and describe the issue, these groups create a contemporary "tower of babble" that fails to adequately address media violence and undermines ways to cope with it. They are *consumers, producers, advocates, experts, politicians,* and *reporters.*

Competing Perspectives and Intellectual Paralysis

Consumers. This group includes parents, kids, adults, and people with whom they interact daily like teachers, counselors, physicians, and clergy. Its agenda is to find coherent information about the potential risks of media violence and easy-to-understand ways to do something about it—like monitoring kids' viewing habits, using the V-Chip, Cybersitter, or Net Nanny.

Producers. Media is a business. The primary agenda in the entertainment and news industries is to attract audiences. Profit making supersedes concerns over ideology, ethics, or the social consequences of media. This perspective generally defends practices in the interest of free speech and a free market, or by asserting that media violence simply reflects today's society.

Advocates. Foundations, advocacy groups, and non-profit organizations like the Children's Defense Fund, the Christian Coalition, and the American Medical Association articulate concerns of consumers in the interest of bringing attention to issues and recommending action or legislation. At times this rhetoric can betray an ideological bias or political agenda.

Experts. Writers and researchers are often cited in the media violence debate with the belief that such "experts" provide objective and unbiased perspectives. But the very nature of expertise is specialization. Hence, experts bring their own perspectives, fields of interest, and varying levels of quality and veracity.

Politicians. Lawmakers, commissions, and candidates for office have clear stakes in appearing responsive to constituents in their defense of public safety and "family values." Often responding to the latest shocking movie or school tragedy, politicians favor hyperbole over sober rhetoric and quick fixes over long-term efforts.

Reporters. Newspapers, magazines, TV, and internet journalists need to convert complex events into easily digested reports. As a consequence reporters often condense, exaggerate, or simply distort research findings, frequently embellishing them with opportunistic commentary from public officials or the anguished reactions of families victimized by violence.

The public appetite for violent imagery across a broad spectrum of formats has firmly established violence as a production staple.

This jumble of competing claims and arguments is enough to confuse even the most discerning reader. The result is a kind of intellectual paralysis that subverts efforts to help the situation. Clearly ways are needed to reconcile the contradictions among these sympathetic, yet methodologically incompatible, groups. . . . Otherwise the discussion will remain mired in polemics and bickering. As one veteran of the field recently wrote, "Although scientific researchers have produced a strong body of evidence demonstrating that exposure to media violence harms society, the evidence has never been translated into practical and accessible ideas."

A Production Staple

The absence of practical plans to address violence is becoming all the more frustrating with the recognition that the perceived problem seems to be escalating. Recent advances in digital-effects technologies, the exploding popularity of computer games, and growing consolidation of profit-driven media conglomerates are pushing violence with unprecedented ferocity. Perhaps not so coincidentally, this is occurring at a historical moment when catastrophes in real life are often barely distinguishable from those created for the screen. The public appetite for violent imagery across a broad spectrum of formats has firmly established violence as a production staple. Besides appealing to the broadest domestic audience demographics, the visual quality of violent fare makes it easily marketable in non-English speaking "after-markets" around the globe. Moreover, movies heavy with digital special effects are now becoming cheap to make. This financial incentive not only drives the selection of what films get made, it increasingly factors in how movies initially are conceived. The same holds true with the burgeoning computer game market, which repeats narrow formulas of pursuit and assault decorated with digital weaponry, gore, and sound. The Kaiser Family Foundation reported in 1999 that most homes with children had video game hardware. Many people argue that the interactive character of games makes them far more potent as "teaching machines" than other media. Such general perceptions, especially as the risks pertain to young children, have been articulated in literature reviews by Lillian Bensley and Juliet Van Eenwyk and by Mark Griffiths. This is why it is so important to look at the economic underpinnings of these industries and the way market forces interact with public demand for violent entertainment on a global scale. Examining these issues helps explain the growing supply of such material and why efforts to stem the tide of violent material have failed.

Selective News Reporting

Then one has to ask why we haven't gotten further in efforts to do something about the overwhelming onslaught of violent imagery. Concern is growing that the escalation in the volume and intensity of representational violence is occurring at a time when the general level of public fear is also rising. As movies, television, and games deliver fictional accounts of terror and disaster, the news media serve up accounts of murder, road rage, gang warfare, workplace violence, drug trafficking, internet porn, plane wrecks, killer moms, and medical malpractice. News—or the news that gets reported—is increasingly driven by spectacle. This is especially the case on television, where network journalism has been losing out to splashier fare from Fox, CNN, MSNBC, and other cable providers. As a consequence, television news is far more likely to feature readily visualized stories of conflict or crime over less telegenic issues like health care or child poverty. The result is a public obsessed about risk and catastrophe far in excess of any real danger. Statistics reveal that there was no epidemic of child abductions [in 2006] and that gun-toting teens are not invading the nation's schools. But what continues to occur to a disturbing degree is what communications specialist George Gerbner has termed the "mean world syndrome," as audiences become convinced over time that life is more dangerous. Not only does this lead to heightened public anxiety, but it also makes recognition less likely of actual dangers to people's lives—like drunk drivers or fast-food burgers. It makes people likely to support reactionary public policies advancing quick fixes for fear rather than those that address the complexity of community concerns. In this way the mean world effect is an impediment to healthy civic discourse.

The Violent Center of the Universe

Until fairly recently much [of the] television, movies, and computer games that featured hyperviolence conveyed the impression that harm strikes outside of suburban America. Violence mostly happens to "someone else." It tells audiences, often inaccurately, that brutality and suffering exist in some faraway place, but not at home. This is what has afforded recent sniper attacks, child abductions, and office bombings such emotionalism; the recognition that bad things don't only happen to other people. Yet contrary to speculation following the [terrorist attacks] of September 11, 2001, that a fearful public would avoid movies and television about "homeland" atrocities, the opposite has occurred. Fed a daily diet of sensationalized news stories and color-coded terrorist attack warnings, the public craving for tales of war and apocalypse has grown, as evidenced by the success of films like *Collateral Damage* (2002), *United 93* (2006), and *World Trade Center* (2006). Connections to the 9/11 events can be quite explicit. Currently, leading computer games among US teenagers include "Splinter Cell," about hidden terrorist cohorts, and "Counterstrike," in which players choose roles as terrorists or counterterrorists.

A "just say no" approach to media violence is no more a solution for consumers than new regimes of government censorship are for producers.

As these narratives circulate within the US, they are exported around the globe by an American media industry that dominates worldwide film and television production. Violent media spectacles enhanced by sophisticated digital effects appeal to the widest demographics and translate most easily across age and language barriers. The profitability of violence drives movie production, television programming, and most computer games, as media corporations compete in developing the most engaging strains of hyperviolence. The violent images that the US sells around the world portray the US and its people as the center of the universe. These productions also tell other nations that America is a forceful, deadly, and unbeatable adversary. This is one of the reasons why the US military often supports the production of movies and television that glorify its war-making abilities.

Narrowly Conceived and Conveyed

Media violence isn't going to disappear and most current efforts to stop it are unlikely to succeed. Like displays of material excess and gratuitous sex, violence exists within a commercial structure predicated on a powerful system of fantasies. Whether or not we like to admit it, these fantasies accrue their appeal and popularity because they are linked to people's deepest desires and fears. Clearly these impulses might be expressed in more productive—or more creative—ways. The issue isn't so much that there is too much violence circulating in the media. It is that the violence we see is so narrowly conceived and conveyed. Big media's need for big audiences and shareholder returns has created a very small view of the world. What we need are more diverse and expansive representations of life with all of its tragedies and violent episodes—as well as its joys and inspirations. Certainly, efforts on a personal level can be made to choose entertainment with discretion, to supervise viewing by children, and to not support offensive material. In institutional terms, important work is being done through media education programs and consumer efforts to hold the media industry to higher standards. But a "just say no" approach to media violence is no more a solution for consumers than new regimes of government censorship are for producers. We need a more open and representative media system that affords variety in production and genuine choice in consumption. The growing popularity of interactive programming available through the internet and digital search-and-record technologies has revived the promise of media diversity once anticipated from cable television. . . .

The issue has been fodder for headline-hungry politicians and religious extremists pandering to the fears of a public often misinformed by distorted news reports and opinion pieces masquerading as fact. Not that intellectuals have done much better. Given the breadth and complexity of the issue, academics working in a variety of disciplines have generated a myriad of contradictory findings and theories. Where one stands in the media violence issue depends very much on what questions are asked and who asks them. Largely lacking in the debate are voices that attempt to combine perspectives from areas like social sciences, film studies, cultural studies, and political economy. Yet unless one considers the media violence question broadly in this way, only a partial understanding of the topic will result.

7

Girls Have Become More Violent

Liz Welch

Liz Welch is a writer based in New York City.

In schools and neighborhoods across the country, fights between girls are becoming so vicious that they are seriously hurting and even killing each other. Girls are punching, choking, and even using knives or other weapons. Experts believe that the new degree of brutality in girls' behavior stems from the recent parade of women as aggressors in movies and television. Others suggest that girls who are prone to violence have been abused or live with constant violence at home. Mainly, physical confrontations between teenage girls—including former friends—are sparked by romantic jealousy, competitiveness, or revenge. So, any girl could potentially find herself in a violent situation with another one.

At 5:45 P.M. on October 11, 2004, 15-year-old Frances Hynds lay in a pool of blood on the sidewalk in her neighborhood in Queens, New York. Tiffany Pelez, 16, had just stabbed her with a 6-inch dagger. Tiffany ran off as her boyfriend, 20-year-old Raymond Almodovar, and friend, 16-year-old Hannah Van Fleet, stood there in shock. Finally, someone called 911. But it was too late—Frances was dead.

The crazy thing is, Tiffany and Frances used to be friends. But they'd been fighting over Raymond for a while. Tiffany was dating him—he had dated Frances a year earlier—and thought that Frances was trying to get him back. Frances denied it but Tiffany didn't believe her, and the two girls were at war. "Ray would call Fran and say, 'I think you're prettier than Tiffany,'" says Olivia Hynds-Tapp, Frances's 22-year-old sister. "Fran told Tiffany, but instead of seeing her as a friend, Tiffany saw her as a threat—and they stopped being friends." Olivia says that Tiffany started sending her sister threatening e-mails and spreading nasty rumors about her at school. Fran was tired of it—and the two girls agreed to meet that day in October to hash things out. It wasn't supposed to get that violent, but things got out of control. Frances and Tiffany started yelling, and Frances pulled out a box cutter—Olivia says she has no idea why her sister brought it to the meeting—and slashed Tiffany just above her ear. As Frances took off running, Hannah allegedly handed Tiffany a dagger and told her to stab Frances. Tiffany grabbed the weapon and ran after her. When she caught up to her, Frances turned around and Tiffany plunged the blade into her former friend's chest.

This Violence Is Not So Unusual

Olivia was stunned when she found out her sister was dead. "When you think of girls fighting, you think of screaming and scratching," she says. "So when my father called me to say that Fran had been stabbed, I didn't believe him." But the sad truth is, Tiffany and Frances's story is not so unusual. In schools all across the country, girls are getting physically violent with one another. Three out of every five girls who responded to a *CosmoGIRL!* Web poll say they have punched or kicked another girl during a fight. And the Office of Juvenile Justice and Delinquency Prevention reports that the number of teenage girls arrested for aggravated assault has risen 82 percent over the past [almost two decades]. The main reason girls are fighting? Guys. "Half of the most serious violent fights between girls are sparked by romantic jealousy, competition, or revenge," says Angela Browne, associate director of the Harvard Youth Violence Prevention Center.

Physical fights among girls are nothing new. What is new is the fact that the fights are so vicious that girls are actually killing each other—as in Tiffany and Frances's case. Why? For one thing, experts say, girls are seeing a lot more women attacking one another in movies and on TV: Angelina Jolie in *Tomb Raider*, Jennifer Garner on *Alias*, and Uma Thurman in the *Kill Bill* movies, to name just a few. While it's definitely empowering for teen girls to see women portrayed as aggressors instead of victims, experts believe the problem is that some girls interpret the trend to mean that fighting is cool and don't understand the real danger involved. "In the movie *Mean Girls*, there's a brawl scene that's meant to be funny," explains Cheryl Dellasega, who founded Club Ophelia, an after-school program based in Hershey, Pennsylvania, that teaches girls how to respond to bullying without fighting. "But it's not funny when real teen girls end up in comas."

Another reason many girls turn violent, says Browne, is because they're either being abused or witnessing violence at home—whether it's at the hands of a parent, a stepparent, or a parent's boyfriend or girlfriend. A girl who lives with violence, she explains, is more likely to be violent. "Girls sometimes are violent against other people because they can't hit back against a scary person at home," Browne says. "For them the world isn't a safe place, so they grow up thinking the best defense is a good offense."

Born to Fight

Seventeen-year-old Jackie Noto grew up in Palatine, Illinois, a middle-class suburb of Chicago. She says her mom suffers from bipolar disorder and has verbally abused her since she was about 13. The high school senior says she never really retaliated against her mom—but now she has a problem controlling herself in other hostile situations. She admits she has a hard time backing down from an argument—and often, that leads to physical violence. "I feel like I always have to be on guard," she says. "As soon as any girl touches me, I see red. I just can't control my anger."

Despite the poor relationship she has with her mom, she still listens to her advice. "My mom has always said, 'If someone lays a hand on you, you have the right to fight back,'" says Jackie. "And that's what I believe—whether it's right or wrong." That attitude has landed her in about 20 fights since middle school. And like Tiffany and Frances's, most of Jackie's fights have been over guys. In eighth grade, she started dating DJ, who was then a sophomore in high school. One night DJ called and told her that Lisa, a girl who liked him, was with him at his friend's house. Jackie had already warned Lisa to stay away from her boyfriend, so she became furious—and went over to confront her. "When I got inside, I asked her why she was there, and she pushed me onto the front porch," says Jackie. Her defensive nature kicked in: She grabbed Lisa and put her in a headlock. Then Lisa bit Jackie on her breast. That's when Jackie threw Lisa over a bush onto her back to end the fight.

While it's definitely empowering for teen girls to see women portrayed as aggressors instead of victims, experts believe ... some girls interpret the trend to mean that fighting is cool.

[In 2003], Jackie's aggression also ruined her relationship with her best friend, Renee. Jackie was sleeping over at her house when Renee, 17, confessed that she'd had sex with Jackie's then-boyfriend. "I couldn't believe it," Jackie says. "I was betrayed by both my best friend and my boyfriend." Jackie was hurt and angry, and she spent the night on the couch. The next morning, she left—and from there, their friendship went downhill until they were barely speaking. Two months later, Renee called Jackie and asked her to meet her in a grocery store parking lot. When Jackie saw her, all the feelings of hurt and anger came flooding back—and she started yelling at her former best friend. When Renee pushed Jackie, she pushed her back. The two girls started shoving each other harder and harder until Jackie fell to the ground and Renee got on top of her and started screaming, "Oh, you're so tough? Look who's on top!" Jackie flipped Renee onto her back, then Renee grabbed Jackie's throat and started choking her. "I couldn't breathe, so I took her head and banged it on the pavement," Jackie recalls. "She was the first person I ever made bleed." While Jackie says that fight in particular broke her heart, she doesn't usually feel bad about her behavior when a fight is over. "Do I feel bad that it came to that?" she asks herself. "Yeah. But she was choking me. What was I supposed to do? I had to defend myself."

It's Easy to Get Sucked In

Jackie is what experts call a frequent fighter. But any girl can end up in a violent situation with another girl. Take Jackie's friend Kristin Lodygowski, also 17. Kristin hates the idea of fighting. "Even yelling makes me nervous," she says. Still, [in June 2004], after she tried to give a good friend some advice, things got ugly. Kristin says her friend Sophia, 16, was hooking up with a lot of guys and was beginning to get a reputation at school, so she called her up to talk about it. "I told her I thought she was degrading herself," Kristin says. "Sophia got mad and started threatening to kick my ass." The next day at school, Kristin heard that Sophia was spreading rumors about her. "She told everyone I was a liar and a slut," she says. Two weeks later, Kristin and Jackie walked into a party and Sophia was there. That's when Kristin decided to confront her. "I was tired of her talking about me," she says, "so I went up to her and said, 'You keep telling everyone you're going to beat my ass. When are you going to do it?'" They went outside, and Kristin pushed Sophia. Then Sophia punched Kristin in the face, knocking her to the ground and falling on top of her.

Kristin struggled to breathe underneath her friend until Jackie came over and pulled Sophia off her. Kristin ended up with a huge gash above her eye that required stitches. A few weeks later, Sophia walked up to Kristin and said, "We're cool, right?" But although the girls agreed not to fight anymore, they are no longer the friends they were. "Once you've been physically violent with a friend, it's hard to forgive and forget," Kristin explains. "And that's sad—because I think Sophia now realizes that I was just trying to be a good friend."

Kristin says she knows now that fighting with Sophia didn't solve anything. In fact, it made things worse. But for many girls, like Jackie, that realization isn't enough to make them stop fighting. "I don't want to be this way, but I can't help it," says Jackie, who wants to go to school to study psychology. "I've been thinking about taking anger management classes to help control my rage. I really do believe you can work out your problems in ways other than fighting. That's what I want to learn how to do."

8

Girls Have Not Become More Violent

Mike Males

Mike Males is the author of Framing Youth: 10 Myths About the Next Generation, *and he taught sociology at the University of California, Santa Cruz.*

Claims that girls have become more violent in recent years are greatly exaggerated. Recent literature alleging that they have reached a "new intensity of meanness" due to a culture that promotes violence, sex, and materialism rely on skewed assertions and out-of-date information. For instance, the commonly cited figure for increased assault arrests for girls is a decade old. Moreover, while violent crimes committed by adults have risen, trends in youth violence have improved. Addressing the small number of severely troubled girls is useful, but youth-bashing authors stigmatize teens on the whole and ignore the far more harmful effects of poverty by blaming pop culture.

Loyola University psychologist and renowned "youth violence" authority James Garbarino's sequel to *Lost Boys* [*See Jane Hit: Why Girls Are Growing More Violent and What We Can Do About It*] laments today's generation of girls, who "have bought into the toxic myth" sold by "ever more nasty and vicious pop culture" messages that "link violence, sex and materialism." Because of "toxic culture," Garbarino argues, girls' greater assertiveness, sports activities, and self-reliance have "unintended consequences": a new "intensity of mean-

Mike Males, "And Now . . . Superpredatrixes?" *Youth Today*, vol. 15, no. 5, May 2006, p. 34. Copyright © 2006 *Youth Today*, published by the American Youth Work Center. Reproduced by permission.

ness" and trends among "girls today [to] assault people and get arrested more often than did girls of generations past."

Garbarino recounts anecdotes illustrating his claim that diminishing parental supervision, "spirit-deadening, superficial materialism," and meanness are "promulgated through the vehicle of pop culture that often undermines legitimate adult authority." He predicts more violence, especially with guns, as cultural images drive girls to be more cruel and "empty inside." He recommends "intervention and treatment," violence prevention, and spiritual development programs targeting girls.

Beyond presenting anecdotes and emotional assertions, does Garbarino really show that girls are becoming more savage?

Girls' murder and robbery arrest rates stand at their lowest levels in 40 years.

I checked his factual claims against such standard references as the FBI, the National Center for Health Statistics (NCHS), the National Crime Victimization Survey (NCVS), and the U.S. Bureau of Justice Statistics (BJS). Garbarino's statistics are mind-numbingly wrong—a junk heap of second-hand, outdated numbers, all slanted in the scariest directions.

Outdated Statistics and Panicky Claims

The chief premise of *See Jane Hit*—that America faces a "recent, dramatic increase in violence by troubled girls"—simply isn't true. FBI and BJS reports show that girls' rates of violent felonies have been declining since 1995, as have their rates of murder and robbery since 1993 and school fights since 1992. Girls' murder and robbery arrest rates stand at their lowest levels in 40 years.

Even amid proliferating "toxic culture," our best crime index, the NCVS, reports 60 percent declines over the past decade in all types of violence suffered and perpetrated by teens of both sexes. In 2004, rates of violence reached their lowest points since the first survey in 1973.

The argument that girls are more violent rests on the decade-old increase in girls' assault arrests. FBI reports I examined show that girls' assault arrests increased from 6,300 in 1981 to a peak of 16,800 in 1995, then dropped to 14,300 in 2004—a 32 percent decline in per capita assault arrest rates in a decade.

So, at best, Garbarino's 2006 book is 10 to 15 years out of date. But there's another complication. If more arrests for assault prove that violence is rising, then mothers are becoming violent twice as fast as their daughters. Among women ages 35 to 54, the same FBI reports show, felony assault arrests rocketed from 7,100 in 1981 to 26,600 in 1995, and continued rising to 28,500 in 2004. Assault arrests among middle-aged men also more than doubled, reaching 106,200 in 2004.

The past assault arrest increase among girls that Garbarino and others trumpet actually occurred among both sexes and all ages and tracked stronger policing of domestic abuse. Why, then, does Garbarino pick on girls and their "toxic culture" while dodging more alarming violence trends among his own, older age groups?

Obviously, young girls are easier to stigmatize, and commentators exploit their powerlessness. *See Jane Hit*, like Deborah Prothrow-Stith's *Sugar and Spice and No Longer Nice* and other cloned teen-panic books, have created a "footnote mill" of slanted, outdated statistics and panicky claims in which authors cite and re-cite each other in a rising spiral of destructive misinformation.

Statistics Work Against Garbarino

"[Around 1981], almost ten boys were arrested for assault for every one girl," Garbarino writes, misstating numbers from Prothrow-Stith. "Now, the ratio is four to one."

Wrong. FBI figures show that [around 1981] five boys were arrested for assault per girl, not 10.

"Juveniles commit about two thousand murders per year . . . about 12 percent of the total murders overall in the United States," Garbarino writes, citing a report for 1990. "Female juveniles commit . . . a bit more than two hundred."

Wrong. The latest FBI reports show juveniles commit 5 percent of the nation's murders, around 800 per year. Girls commit around 75.

"Now, girls are . . . cutting and stabbing, poisoning and shooting themselves, in record numbers," Garbarino writes (citing another 1990s report that is outdated and cites a temporary suicide rise that ended two decades ago). ". . . From 1981 to 1998, the suicide rate for girls increased seven percent."

Wrong. The latest NCHS figures show the suicide rate for girls declined 10 percent from 1981 to 1998 and fell another 17 percent from 1998 through 2003. Gun suicides among girls plummeted from 233 in 1981 to 88 in 2003. "I have seen boys who would have fought with fists and knives thirty years ago just as readily take up guns today," Garbarino declares. "I have known sixteen-year-olds who would have agonized over whether or not to kiss on the first date thirty years ago today nonchalantly report on their multiple sex partners."

Nonsensical asides like this tell us more about the author than about teens. If, as Garbarino intends us to believe, his impressions reflect real trends among youth, we'd expect to see explosions in murder, pregnancy, and sexually transmitted infections like gonorrhea and syphilis among teens. Yet, the most recent FBI and health statistics (which he never bothered to check) show that rates of all three are sharply lower among youth today than among youth of 30 years ago.

Tarring an Entire Generation

Despite improving trends, the annual Monitoring the Future report finds that 10 percent of girls are unhappy with themselves, 10 percent feel unsafe, and 5 percent feel alienated from their peers. BJS reports that 7 percent are bullied at school.

Garbarino provides useful insights for addressing the fraction of severely troubled girls, although his rush to blame pop culture for everything ignores the far more devastating effects of poverty. Rates of violence and murder are four to seven times higher among black girls than white girls.

Authors and commentators popularize themselves by incessantly disparaging young people with cruel stereotypes.

Garbarino could have accomplished his worthy goals without tarring an entire generation with the few disturbed youths he sees professionally and in sensational news stories. Studies by Northwestern University psychiatrist Daniel Offer find that psychologists and other health professionals drastically overestimate the pathology suffered by normal teens.

Garbarino, like other authors in today's youth-bashing herd, expresses disdain for younger generations: "Mean girls" are now the "dominant force . . . in peer groups"; boys "are as bad as they can get"; teen peers are "usually a negative influence"; youths are passive imitators of pop-culture depravities unless adults "rescue them."

Like the "alpha girls" deplored in such popular books as Rachel Simmons' *Odd Girl Out* or Cheryl Delasegga's *Girl Wars*, authors and commentators popularize themselves by incessantly disparaging young people with cruel stereotypes miscast as "scientific findings," mean gossip couched in phony statistics and demeaning assertions, and by smugly glossing over their own deficiencies. If this isn't "social toxicity," I don't know what is.

9

Stricter Gun Control Laws Can Prevent Youth Violence

Children's Defense Fund

Children's Defense Fund (CDF) is a not-for-profit children's advocacy group based in Washington, D.C.

In 2005, the year after Congress allowed the Assault Weapons Ban to end, the number of children and teens killed by firearms increased for the first time since 1994. And while the recent shootings at Virginia Tech and Northern Illinois University outraged the public, the epidemic of gun violence that kills young people across the country every day goes unnoticed. To protect children and teens, citizens must elect public officials who will enact stricter gun control laws. Congress must also take legislative action to require background checks on those who purchase guns from unlicensed dealers, especially at gun shows.

According to the most recent data from the Centers for Disease Control and Prevention, 3,006 children and teens were killed by firearms in 2005, the first increase since 1994 and the first rise in gun deaths since Congress allowed the Assault Weapons Ban to expire in 2004.

When 32 people were killed at Virginia Tech and five at Northern Illinois University, the public was outraged. Yet every four days we have the equivalent of a Virginia Tech tragedy that passes unnoticed. Our gun violence epidemic robs parents of their children, wastes our human potential, and drains resources from our health care system.

What is it going to take for us to stop this senseless loss of young lives? We need to ensure that those we elect to public office enact legislation that will really protect children by limiting the number of guns in our communities, controlling who can obtain firearms and the conditions of their use. Individuals and communities must act to end the culture of violence that desensitizes us, young and old, to the value of life.

The Statistics Are Startling

We cannot allow these shots to go unheard. Our children and our society deserve no less.

- The number of children and teens in America killed by guns in 2005 would fill 120 public school classrooms of 25 students each.

- In 2005, 69 preschoolers were killed by firearms compared to 53 law enforcement officers killed in the line of duty.

- Since 1979, gun violence has snuffed out the lives of 104,419 children and teens in America. Sixty percent of them were White; 37 percent were Black.

- The number of Black children and teens killed by gunfire since 1979 is more than 10 times the number of Black citizens of all ages lynched in American history.

- The number of children and teens killed by guns since 1979 would fill 4,177 public school classrooms of 25 students each.

The latest data from the U.S. Centers for Disease Control and Prevention show that 3,006 children and teen died from gunfire in the United States in 2005—one child or teen every three hours, eight every day, 58 children and teens every week.

- 1,972 were homicide victims

- 822 committed suicide

- 212 died in accidental or undetermined circumstances

- 2,654 were boys

- 352 were girls

- 404 were under age 15

- 131 were under age 10

- 69 were under age 5

- 1,624 were White

- 1,271 were Black

- 614 were Latino

- 60 were Asian or Pacific Islander

- 51 were American Indian or Alaska Native

More than five times as many children and teens suffered non-fatal gun injuries.

Did You Know?

- 181 more children and teens died from firearms in 2005 than in 2004—the first annual increase since 1994.

- 168 more children and teens died from homicide in 2005 than in 2004.

- 56 more White, 122 more Black, 40 more Hispanic, and 9 more Asian and Pacific Islander children and teens died in 2005 than in 2004.

- More 10- to 19-year-olds die from gunshot wounds than from any other cause except motor vehicle accidents.

- Almost 90 percent of the children and teens killed by firearms in 2005 were boys.

- Black children and teens are more likely to be victims of firearm homicide. White children and teens are more likely to commit suicide.

- The firearm death rate for Black males ages 15 to 19 is more than four times that of comparable White males.

- A Black male has a 1 in 72 chance of being killed by a firearm before his 30th birthday; a White male has a 1 in 344 chance.

- Eight times as many White children and teens committed suicide by gun as Black children and teens.

- Males ages 15 to 19 are almost eight times as likely as females that age to commit suicide with a firearm.

Removing guns from the home is one of the best ways to protect children and teens from gun deaths.

We Can Protect Children and Teens from Gun Violence

To confront America's deadly, historic romance with guns and violence and protect children from firearms in their homes, schools, communities and nation, you can:

1. *Support Common Sense Gun Safety Measures.* Because federal law requires criminal background checks *only* for guns sold through licensed firearm dealers, 40 percent of all firearms in the United States are purchased *without* a background check, including those bought at gun shows. Congress must enact legislation that closes the gun show loophole by requiring criminal background checks on those who purchase guns from unlicensed gun dealers. Six states require background checks on all firearm purchases and others require them only for handguns, but

35 states have no laws that affect the gun show loop-hole. Contact your elected officials to express your views on the need for gun measures to protect children. Call the White House at (202) 456-1414 or your members of Congress at (202) 224-3121.

2. *Remove Guns from Your Home.* There are over 200 million firearms in the United States, including more than 65 million handguns. Reports have shown that the presence of guns in the home increases the risk of homicide and suicide. Removing guns from the home is one of the best ways to protect children and teens from gun deaths.

3. *Stress Nonviolent Values and Conflict Resolution.* Family violence is epidemic, child abuse and neglect are widespread, and children are being continuously exposed to television programming crammed with scenes of brutality. Concerned citizens along with schools and churches must organize nonviolent conflict resolution support groups in their communities. Excellent resources include: Dr. Deborah Prothrow-Stith's *Peace by Piece: A Guide for Preventing Community Violence* and "Violence Prevention Curriculum for Adolescents," as well as "Resolving Conflict Creatively" by Linda Lantieri, co-author of *Waging Peace in Our Schools*, available on the Educators for Social Responsibility website at www.esrnational.org.

4. *Refuse to Buy or Use Products for Children and Teens That Glamorize Violence.* Our culture frequently glamorizes guns and violence in movies, television shows, music and on the Internet. Many shows targeted at children contain violent themes and language. Protest and refuse to buy or use products that glamorize violence or make it socially acceptable or fun. Turn off violent programming and read with your children instead.

5. *Raise Awareness of Child and Teen Gun Deaths and Injuries.* What you can do:

- Urge local newspapers and radio and television stations to publish and broadcast photographs of children and teens killed in your community.

- Encourage the reading at your place of worship of the names of children and teens in your community killed by guns and publish their photos in your congregational bulletin.

- Write a letter to the editor or an op-ed piece about the tragic loss of young lives to gun violence.

6. *Invite Community Leaders to Witness the Effects of Gun Violence for Themselves.* Organize a "Child Watch[SM]" visit for influential members of your community to see firsthand the effects of gun violence. Ask your local hospital to arrange visits with medical teams that can share their experiences of dealing with the victims and families impacted by gun violence.

7. *Provide Children and Teens Positive Alternatives to the Streets Where They Can Feel Safe and Protected.* Gangs, drugs, and guns are available to many children seven days a week, 24 hours a day. We must offer positive alternatives and role models to children during after-school hours, weekends, and summers. We need to open our congregational, school and community doors and engage them in purposeful activities. Check CDF's [Children's Defense Fund's] Web site at www.childrensdefense.org/freedomschools for more information about the CDF Freedom Schools® reading and enrichment model, which includes nonviolence training.

10

Gun Control Laws Cannot Prevent Youth Violence

Howard Nemerov

Howard Nemerov frequently appears as Analyst at Large on nu-merous radio shows and is the Austin Gun Rights Examiner at Examiner.com. Nemerov is also the author of Four Hundred Years of Gun Control: Why Isn't It Working?

Stricter gun control laws would not prevent violence among and against children and teens. In fact, firearm-related injuries and homicides of youths are only part of the bigger picture. For example, while firearm-related deaths of persons 20 and younger increased in 2005 after the Assault Weapons Ban expired, fatal-ity rates in other categories, such as drowning and being struck, saw increases as well. Furthermore, gun control organizations ig-nore the deaths of children that are attributed to neglect and abuse even though they outstrip deaths by firearms. Ultimately, unnecessary gun control laws inhibit adults' ability to protect themselves and others, including youths.

The death of a child is horrible and painful, and any decent person would do whatever it takes to save that life. How could an organization called the Children's Defense Fund (CDF) possibly have an agenda that could result in more child fatalities?

A recent report by the CDF leads with: "Firearm Deaths Among Children and Teens Increase for the First Time Since

1994: 3,006 in 2005." Insisting this ties into the now-defunct Clinton "assault weapons" ban, CDF says:

> According to the most recent data from the Centers for Disease Control and Prevention [CDC], 3,006 children and teens were killed by firearms in 2005, the first increase since 1994 and the first rise in gun deaths since Congress allowed the Assault Weapons Ban to expire in 2004.

Gun control organizations often insinuate that the assault weapons ban caused a decline in violent crime, but violent crime peaked in 1991 with an overall rate of 758.2 (per 100,000 population), while the murder rate peaked at 9.8. By 1994, when the "assault weapons" ban went into effect, violent crime dropped 5.9% and murder decreased 8.2%.

The Children's Defense Fund is correct on one point: The CDC reports that, for persons under age 20, the overall firearms death rate rose 5.8% for the 2004–5 time period. However, other categories saw increases as well: The drowning death rate rose 5.3% and struck by/against rate rose 21.8%. It is also important to note that since 1994, the drowning death rate decreased 19.8% and struck by/against dropped 20.1%, while the firearms death rate declined 52.0%. These data illustrate how one year's data trend may vary from the longer trend. This is why, in response to the preliminary report that crime decreased in 2007 after a two-year increase, an FBI spokesman stated: "One preliminary report does not make a trend. . ."

Real 'Child' Mortality Data

The Children's Defense Fund claims increasing gun control will save children's lives:

> We need to ensure that those we elect to public office enact legislation that will really protect children by limiting the number of guns in our communities, controlling who can obtain firearms and the conditions of their use.

Another gambit by gun control organizations is to include older teens and adults in their calculations, in order to produce . . . a scarier number, implying that eight children a day die because "gun lovers" only care about "their rights."

Oxford English Dictionary defines the word "childhood" as: "the time from birth to puberty." Oxford defines "puberty" as: "The period during which adolescents reach sexual maturity and become capable of reproduction. . ." In terms of age, there seems to be general agreement that this ability to procreate occurs by the age of 15.

In 2005, the total firearms death rate for CDF's "children and teens" was 3.70. However, the rate for those age 18–19 was 18.56, and the rate for those age 15–17 was 8.50. For true children (age 0–14) the rate was 1.31; 404 children were killed by firearms in 2005 for all intents, an average of slightly over one per day.

The U.S. Health and Human Services estimates that in 2005, 1,460 children died as a result of abuse and neglect (4 each day, 1.96 per 100,000 population); 76.6% of that total was younger than four years old. Infant boys (younger than 1 year) had the highest fatality rate at 17.3, followed by infant girls at 14.5; 79.4% of the perpetrators were parents. Curiously, CDF's *Programs* page includes no child abuse/neglect initiative, even though over three times as many children were killed by abuse/neglect than by firearms.

Furthermore, the CDC reports there were 230 child firearm homicides in 2005, but there were 1,022 total child homicides. This means that 77.5% of all child homicides occurred without using a gun. Meanwhile, the victims of 87.1% of all drowning homicides, 88.1% of all poisoning homicides, and 66.7% of all suffocation homicides were children—physically less able to fend off an attacker. The idea that someone *needs* a gun to kill a child is naïve.

According to the CDC, between 1994 and 2005, the overall homicide rate for children decreased by 28.2%, but their firearms homicide rate dropped 53.0%. The overall child fatal injury rate decreased 26.6%, but the overall firearms fatal injury rate dropped 55.9%. The overall accidental injury rate for children dropped 28.1%, but the accidental firearms death rate, already a miniscule 0.32 per 100,000 children, decreased 61.4% to 0.12 per 100,000. During this same time period, the firearms homicide rate for the U.S. non-child population (age 15 and over) decreased 38.0% and the accidental fatal firearms injury rate dropped 46.8%. Children experienced a better-than-average decrease in fatality rates across the board compared to the general population. Children started out safer in 1994 and became even safer through 2005.

Nor do children need firearms to kill themselves. In 2005, 84 children committed suicide using a firearm, all of them in the 10–14 age range. Two children age 5–9 intentionally suffocated themselves. There were 272 total child suicides; 69.1% of these occurred by non-firearm means. There were 5,162 accidental child deaths in 2005; 1.5% of them (75) involved firearms. Between 1994 and 2005, children's overall suicide rate decreased 19.6%, but their firearms suicide rate dropped 57.5%. This compares favorably to the total population's experience of a 7.0% lower overall suicide rate and 19.6% lower firearms suicide rate.

Considering that during this time period the Bureau of Alcohol, Tobacco, Firearms and Explosives estimated an average of 4.5 million new firearms were sold each year, there is either no correlation—or a negative one (more guns, lower death rate)—between civilian firearms inventory and fatal firearms injuries.

The 1994–2005 decrease in children's fatal firearms injuries outstripped every category except for cut/pierce, which declined 57.2%. Poisoning deaths decreased only 5.9% and struck by/against declined 7.9%. Suffocation death rates for children *increased* 34.3%. CDF's *Publications* page prominently features their gun control report, but there are no publications that [focus] on reducing poisoning or suffocation fatalities.

The Other Side of the Equation

The problem with organizations that represent only one side of an issue is that their intentional lack of context creates misleading distortions. When discussing the emotionally intense subject of child fatalities, such distortions can lead to promoting policies which 'feel good' but produce negative consequences.

In the Supreme Court case of *District of Columbia v. Heller*, CDF signed onto an amicus brief in support of the D.C. gun ban, which since 1976 has effectively banned all functioning firearms. The CDC reports that for the years of 1999–2005, the national homicide rate for children was 1.76, while the rate in D.C. was higher than any state at 5.82. For the years 1994–1998, the national children's homicide rate was 2.14, but D.C. again led all states at 8.76.

Moreover, the national firearms homicide rate for children between 1999 and 2005 was 0.40, but the rate was 1.46 under the D.C. gun ban. The national non-firearms homicide rate for children during this time period was 1.36, lower than the *firearms* homicide rate in D.C. The non-firearms homicide rate in D.C. between 1999 and 2005 was 4.37, higher than the total child homicide rate for the entire country. These data underline the fact that availability of guns has no correlation with child homicide rates.

Sergio Aguilar didn't need a firearm to murder his own son, whom he believed had "demons" that required violent exorcism:

A 27-year-old grocery store worker who police say punched and kicked his 2-year-old son to death on a country road calmly told motorists who stopped at the scene that he had to "get the demons" out of the boy, two witnesses said Monday.

When unarmed witnesses tried to stop him, his violent demeanor stymied their efforts:

> "What we got from witnesses is he was punching, slapping, kicking, stomping, shaking," [police spokesman] Singh said. "They tried to intervene and get involved, but their efforts really didn't have an effect ... He just pushed them off and went back to it."

Witnesses called law enforcement, but it was too late to save the baby:

> And when a Modesto police officer jumped off a helicopter and ordered Aguiar [sic] to stop at gunpoint, he raised his middle finger and continued his attack.

> Officer Jerry Ramar, standing in a cow pasture behind an electric fence, shot Aguiar [sic] once in the forehead, the witnesses and police said. Aguiar [sic] died at the scene.

> "Good shot, thank God," said Deborah McKain, a 51-year-old resident of nearby Crows Landing ... "That guy needed to die."

With few exceptions, law-abiding California residents can't carry concealed handguns. What if an armed citizen had shot Aguilar instead [of] waiting for the police to arrive? If it saves a child's life, it's worth it, right?

In the last two months, media reported numerous self-defense stories where armed parents protected their children from violent criminals. One homeowner shot two men who had forced their way into his home. Police were "especially concerned because children also live in the home," reasonable apprehension since the invaders stabbed the homeowner before being shot.

A burglar's two-day crime spree ended when his most recent victim shot him with a handgun. The young daughter was home alone, but an alert neighbor called the father, who arrived home in time. "I'm a dad. Any dad would have done the same thing."

When his pregnant wife, home alone with their two-year-old, called to tell him someone was lurking outside, Brian Stevens rushed home. After hearing noise outside, he got his handgun and waited for the police. The burglar entered, and Stevens repeatedly warned him to leave. When the burglar kept advancing, Stevens shot him.

Crime costs society. Guns in the hands of law-abiding people stop crime. Rates of child firearms homicide, suicide, and accidental death are falling faster than the national rates. Laws touted as being "for the children" today risk costing more children's lives tomorrow. Children's Defense Fund would save more children by skipping the social engineering and returning to their core mission of promoting programs which serve the children.

11

Views Differ on Zero Tolerance Policies

Tobin McAndrews

Tobin McAndrews has written articles for ERIC Clearinghouse on Educational Management.

The intent of zero tolerance policies is to deter school violence through automatic suspension or expulsion. Support for zero tolerance varies among different groups and organizations. Advocates claim that strict sanctions are needed to protect students, and public support appears strong for such measures when applied to "persistent troublemakers." Others propose that schools seek alternatives to expulsion, use procedures that are more "child friendly," and oppose zero tolerance policies that are discriminatory. However, some common themes appear, including the call for sound discretion and the use of zero tolerance as part of a comprehensive approach to school safety.

Responding to concern over school safety, state legislatures and school boards in recent years have enacted a range of zero-tolerance policies focused on combating weapons, drugs, violence, and antisocial behavior. Results have been mixed, with some critics discounting the policies altogether. Almost all schools report having zero-tolerance policies for firearms (94 percent) and weapons other than firearms (91 percent), according to the National Center for Education Statistics (Kaufman and others 2000). Eighty-seven percent of schools have zero-tolerance policies for alcohol, and 88 percent have policies for drugs. Most schools also have zero-tolerance policies for violence and tobacco (79 percent each).

This Digest describes the origins of zero-tolerance policies, presents evidence on their effectiveness, examines criticisms of them, and recommends strategies to make the policies more useful.

What Is Zero Tolerance?

Zero-tolerance policies are administrative rules intended to address specific problems associated with school safety and discipline. In 1994 Congress passed the Gun-Free Schools Act, which required states to legislate zero-tolerance laws or risk losing federal funds (Martin 2000). In response, various states, counties, and districts have developed their own policies in tune with local needs. In implementing the policies, some administrators have cast a broad net, treating both minor and major incidents with equal severity to "send a message" to potential violators (Skiba and Peterson 1999).

The Gun-Free Schools Act included language allowing local review on a case-by-case basis. Some administrators have declined to exercise this discretion, believing instead that continued unwavering application of zero tolerance is necessary to deal with disruptive students (Skiba and Peterson).

Sometimes even exemplary students are caught in the zero-tolerance net. For instance, during the 1997-8 school year, a teacher observed 12-year-old Adam L., an A student, filing his nails with a miniature Swiss Army knife; for violating the school's anti-weapons policy, the youth received a one-year expulsion (Zirkel 1999).

Why Were Zero-Tolerance Policies Established?

Zero-tolerance policies were enacted to combat the seemingly overwhelming increase in school violence during the 1990s. In a 1995 School Crime Victimization Survey, 12 percent of responding students knew someone who had brought a gun to school (Ashford 2000). As the media focused on violence in schools, pressure increased on legislators to take action against weapons in schools.

Following enactment of the Gun-Free Schools Act, all 50 states adopted some variation of the law. This law made Elementary and Secondary Education Act (ESEA) funds "contingent on a state's enacting a 'zero-tolerance' law with the goal of producing gun-free schools" (Ashford). Some states went beyond this focus on guns and decided to apply zero tolerance to the entire breadth of possible disciplinary infractions in an effort to weed out violators and standardize discipline.

Are Zero-Tolerance Policies Fulfilling Their Purpose?

It has been almost a decade since schools first began to institute zero-tolerance policies, and more than six years since the Gun-Free Schools Act. Critics claim there has been no concerted effort to test the efficacy of interventions that target school behavior, and few studies have evaluated the effectiveness of zero-tolerance strategies (Skiba and Peterson).

The National Center for Education Statistics found that, after four years of implementation, zero-tolerance policies had little effect at previously unsafe schools; the center also reports that the current data do not demonstrate a dramatic decrease in school-based violence in recent years (Ashford). The popularity of zero-tolerance policies may have less to do with their actual effect than the image they portray of schools taking resolute measures to prevent violence. Whether the policies actually change student behavior may be less important than the reassurance it gives the school community at large (Ashford).

Some schools report positive results from their policies. In Tacoma, Washington, Henry Foss Senior High School's School-Centered Decision Making (SCDM) team implemented in fall

1991 a zero-tolerance policy against fighting. After one year, the policy resulted in a 95 percent drop in violent behavior on campus. Moreover, the policy's positive impact led to record-breaking freshmen enrollment; the majority of new entrants indicated that they were attending the school primarily because of its safety (Burke and Herbert 1996).

Similar results were found in New Jersey's Lower Camden County Regional High School District, where zero tolerance contributed to a 30 percent drop in superintendent disciplinary hearings; drug-related offenses dropped by nearly one-half (Schreiner 1996).

Why Are Zero-Tolerance Policies Criticized?

Zero-tolerance policies create long-term problems through exclusion, say critics. Consistently, school suspension was found to be a moderate to strong predictor of a student's dropping out of school (Skiba and Peterson). When students are not in school, they are on the streets and, more often than not, getting in more serious trouble than they could at school. Setting these policies in stone without any thought to the inherent ambiguities of human interaction allows only arbitrariness and exclusion and, thus, abandons the educational mission of schools, asserts Perlstein (2000).

Zero-tolerance policies have undoubtedly created legal headaches for some school administrators. By greatly increasing the number of students considered for expulsion, and by removing the flexibility previously accorded to administrators, these policies have hindered administrators' ability to address marginal incidents, says Stader (2000).

Perhaps the biggest problem with zero-tolerance policies is inconsistent application and interpretation. David Day, general counsel for four Indiana school districts, says he expects lawsuits when board members suddenly announce they are imposing a zero-tolerance policy that leaves no room for administrators' discretion or students' due-process rights (Jones 2000).

In February 2001, the American Bar Association approved a resolution opposing "policies that have a discriminatory effect, or mandate either expulsion or referral of students to juvenile or criminal court, without regard to the circumstances or nature of the offense or the student's history."

A report on the resolution noted the disproportionate number of African-American students who have been expelled (Juvenile Law Center 2000).

A weak link in the chain connecting policy to practice is that those responsible for implementation often haven't heard of, or don't clearly understand, the policy. In the absence of training on how to deal with infractions, administrative ignorance or ineptitude is largely to blame for lawsuits over disciplinary actions.

Although most mainstream students live in a "one-strike-you're-out" environment, the situation is different for special-education students. Laws governing violations by special-education students generally guarantee the student's right to due process under the Fourteenth Amendment. To expel a special-education student, a panel must be convened to determine whether the violation is related to the student's disability, in which case the school must follow due-process procedures, including an IEP meeting and subsequent hearing (Zirkel).

Special-education students are also protected by the "stay put" provision, which keeps them in their present educational environment unless a court grants a preliminary injunction declaring that the student presents a high level of danger as defined in *Honig v. Doe* (1988).

What Are The Elements Of An Effective Policy?

When formulating a zero-tolerance policy, it may be useful for state officials and local school boards to attend to the following recommendations:

- Specify clear consequences for misbehavior, with consistency of application.

- Allow flexibility and consider expulsion alternatives.

- Clearly define what constitutes a weapon, a drug, or an act of misbehavior.

- Comply with state due-process laws and allow for student hearings.

- Develop the policy collaboratively with all stake-holding agencies (for example, state departments of education, juvenile justice, and health and human services).

- Learn from the experiences educators have had with zero tolerance in other states, schools, and districts.

- Integrate comprehensive health-education programs that include drug and alcohol curricula.

- Tailor the policy to local needs.

- Review the policy each year.

A sound policy allows administrators some degree of discretion in responding to infractions. The policy should allow officials to consider the special circumstances of a violation, such as the age of the offender, the ability of the offender to comprehend the policy, the intent of the offender, the effect of the transgression on other students (both those directly and indirectly involved), and, finally, the past disciplinary record of the offender (Martin). Special circumstances can be used to consider alternatives that may be more appropriate than expulsion.

By categorizing violations in accordance with their severity, administrators send a strong message that violations will not be allowed, while avoiding a "one size fits all" approach (Ashford). While setting up discretionary systems to handle policy violation may prolong the decision-making process, it will free schools from a tangle of due-process litigation and allow decisions to be made on the basis of facts so [that] appropriate disciplinary action can be levied (Stader).

When students are suspended or expelled, they should be referred to outside counseling and, in extreme cases, to local law-enforcement agencies. By following these guidelines, administrators will not only cover their own accountability but also create excellent resources that could offer valuable second opinions into any administrative decisions being made.

A zero-tolerance policy is but one part of a broader set of policies dealing with school safety. Each school district should also develop a crisis-management plan tailored to individual schools and their communities. Conflict-mediation programs, active recruitment of students to participate in planning, and peer mentoring may open lines of communication between students, improve the school climate, and reduce violence (Stader). This strategy has worked for schools in Wisconsin and North Carolina (Blair 1999).

When communicating zero-tolerance policies to the public as well as to the school community, officials should focus on three points: exact definitions of punishable offenses, consequences for noncompliance, and the decision process that will be followed when offenses occur. To alleviate apprehension [reduce anxiety], administrators can stress that children are actually safer at school than anywhere else.

Resources

Ashford, Roger. "Can Zero Tolerance Keep Our Schools Safe?" *Principal* (November 2000): 28–30.

Blair, Frank. "Does Zero Tolerance Work?" *Principal* 79, 1 (September 1999): 36–37. EJ 592 961.

Burke, Ethelda, and Don Herbert. "Zero Tolerance Policy: Combating Violence in Schools." *NASSP Bulletin* (April 1996): 49–54. EJ 522 765.

Jones, Rebecca. "Schools and the Law: Legal Trouble Spots and How to Avoid Them." *American School Board Journal* 187, 4 (April 2000): 24–30. EJ 603 262.

Juvenile Law Center. Philadelphia. For text of American Bar Association resolution, go to http://www.jlc.org/home/updates/updates_links/aba_zerotol.htm.

Kaufman, Philip, and others. "Indicators of School Crime and Safety, 2000." Washington, D.C.: National Center for Education Statistics. *NCES Report* (January 2000): Appendix A, 133–34. ED 444 270.

Martin, Michael. "Does Zero Mean Zero?" *American School Board Journal* 187, 3 (March 2000): 39–41. EJ 601 206.

Perlstein, Daniel. "Failing at Kindness: Why Fear of Violence Endangers Children." *Educational Leadership* (March 2000): 76–79.

Schreiner, Michael. "Bold Steps Build Safe Havens." *School Business Affairs* 62, 11 (November 1996): 44–46. EJ 535 678.

Skiba, Russ, and Reece Peterson. "The Dark Side of Zero Tolerance." *Phi Delta Kappan* 80, 5 (January 1999): 372–76, 381–82. EJ 579 414.

Stader, David. "Preempting Threats with a Sound School Policy." *NASSP Bulletin* 84, 617 (September 2000): 68–72.

Zirkel, Perry. "Zero Tolerance Expulsions." *NASSP Bulletin* 83, 610 (November 1999): 101–05. EJ 597 055.

12

Zero Tolerance Policies Are Unfair

Rhonda B. Armistead

Rhonda B. Armistead is president of the National Association of School Psychologists (NASP), and she is a school psychologist in Charlotte, North Carolina.

Initially used to address weapons-based violence and substance abuse in schools, zero-tolerance policies have been extended to sexual harassment, bullying, and dress code violations. However, this one-size-fits-all approach does not take child development, individual needs, and underlying causes of problem behaviors into account. As a result, students are unfairly punished for minor infractions, leading to dramatic rises in suspensions, expulsions, and arrests, which are counterproductive and drain financial resources. Schools should re-evaluate and revise zero-tolerance policies as well as seek programs that reinforce appropriate decision-making and conflict-resolving skills and examine students' motivations behind misconduct.

A 1st grader is disciplined for "sexual harassment" after smacking a classmate's bottom on the playground and the police are called in; a high school student is expelled after a butter knife brought to school accidentally falls out of her locker; a 17-year-old is arrested and expelled for shooting a paper clip with a rubber band.

Few policies in education have proven to be as universally ineffective—even counterproductive—as "zero tolerance."

Rhonda B. Armistead, "Zero Tolerance: The School Woodshed," *Education Week*, vol. 27, no. 41, June 11, 2008, pp. 24–26. Reproduced by permission.

Brought to prominence in 1994 when Congress enacted the Gun-Free Schools Act to address weapons-based school violence and drug problems, zero-tolerance edicts have become the virtual woodshed of school discipline: They are solely punitive, and lack any positive connection to schools' primary purpose—learning and development.

A zero-tolerance program's goal is to act as a deterrent and provide swift intervention for misconduct, sending a strong, "one strike and you're out" message to students. It prescribes non-negotiable punishment (typically, suspension or expulsion) for a specified behavior, regardless of the extent or context of the infraction. Possession of a butter knife and possession of a switchblade, for instance, automatically receive the same punishment, even though common sense indicates a different intention and degree of risk in the two infractions.

Zero-tolerance policies are associated with declines in academic achievement and increases in student misconduct, school dropouts, and poor attitudes toward adults.

A One-Size-Fits-All Framework

Such a one-size-fits-all framework seriously limits administrators' use of their professional judgment in a given situation, and often forces them to impose punishments they otherwise feel are inappropriate to the facts. It also fails to take into account the intricacies of child development, individual characteristics, risk factors, and underlying causes, all of which shape behavior.

Despite the zero-tolerance concept's shortcomings, however, states and school districts have extended its reach beyond weapons and drugs, to include an array of behaviors, such as sexual harassment, bullying, and dress-code violations. School officials have been responding to legitimate concerns over tragedies such as the Columbine High School shootings, and to increases in youth violence generally. And they have raised the zero-tolerance banner in part as a shield against potential liability. But far from achieving their intended goal of improved behavior and safety, schools are now struggling with the unintended consequences of applying such draconian discipline so broadly. Press reports regularly focus on the absurd extremes to which zero tolerance can be stretched. But a deeper, more pervasive problem lies in the consequent increase in negative outcomes plaguing most schools today.

According to reports from groups such as the American Bar Association and the American Psychological Association, zero-tolerance policies are associated with declines in academic achievement and increases in student misconduct, school dropouts, and poor attitudes toward adults. Research also links zero tolerance to a dramatic rise in suspensions and expulsions and to more frequent referrals to the juvenile-justice system for infractions once handled in schools. Although the policy has been presented as a way to improve school climate, its byproduct of higher rates of suspension and expulsion is associated with less satisfactory ratings of climate and disproportionately greater time spent by schools on disciplinary matters.

Transferring treatable behavior problems to the juvenile-justice system also has economic consequences. The anticrime organization Fight Crime: Invest in Kids has noted that the cost of keeping a child in juvenile detention for one year runs from $35,000 to $50,000, compared with $12,000 to $15,000 per year for prevention and intervention programs. Moreover, for each young person kept from adopting a life of crime, the country saves an estimated $1.7 million.

A Return to the Zero-Tolerance Principle

In an era in which education policy rightly emphasizes reliance on evidence-based strategies, the data should speak for themselves. It is time for zero-tolerance policies to be re-evaluated and revised.

To start, we should stop allowing the punitive *policy* of zero tolerance to co-opt the protective *principle* of zero tolerance, which is an essential underpinning of safe and supportive schools. Schools should never tolerate behavior that disrupts, disrespects, threatens, or harms others. Bullying is not just "kids being kids." Smacking a classmate's bottom, even without sexual intent, is not appropriate playground behavior. The sooner and more directly we address even small infractions with appropriate interventions, the better. But it is important to keep in mind that the primary objective of discipline is to help children learn from their mistakes.

Discipline should teach students appropriate decisionmaking and behavior, as well as a rational relationship between actions and consequences. This starts with clearly defining behavioral expectations and then reinforcing these with skills development. Where students need direct instruction and skills development in interpersonal relations or conflict resolution, the school community needs to make a commitment to embed instruction in these social skills directly in the curriculum. Positive Behavioral Support is one type of evidence-based prevention program being successfully implemented in many schools nationwide.

Misbehavior is also full of "teachable moments" effective discipline programs can use to advantage. These include giving students direct feedback about the appropriateness of their behavior and providing opportunities for modeling, guided practice, and critical feedback. We also need to make sure that we are teaching the desired lesson. For the 1st grader who smacked his classmate's bottom, the lesson is "we don't hit in play or in anger," or "how else can you get a friend's attention?" Defining the behavior as sexual harassment is irrelevant and introduces a concept that a 7-year-old is developmentally unprepared to understand.

Equally important is ensuring that consequences are proportionate to the misconduct. Children and youths care deeply about fairness. Excessive punishment teaches them to mistrust the decisionmaking system and the adults who run it.

Students' Unique Motivations Matter

Perhaps the most overlooked facet of effective discipline is identifying and addressing the underlying cause of the misconduct. This includes understanding the student's developmental level, the motivation and reasoning behind the misconduct, environmental factors, implications of the behavior, resulting outcomes, and how the misconduct is working to help the student either get or avoid something. These considerations are at the heart of "functional behavior assessment," a technique required by federal law before suspending or expelling a student with disabilities and that can be helpful for all students. Its goal is to determine the consequence or disciplinary action that is most likely to decrease future occurrences of the misconduct.

A student with severe performance anxiety might start a fight the day before an oral presentation, for example, knowing that the punishment will be suspension. Getting out of the presentation thus becomes more important than staying out of trouble. Disciplining this student is unlikely to work if it only addresses the symptom—the misconduct—and not the underlying cause. Brief counseling with the school psychologist or counselor is an alternative that could address both the poor judgment involved in starting a fight and the performance anxiety that prompted it.

Does this mean that discipline should never include serious consequences? Absolutely not. But punishment should be balanced with learning. We need policies that allow administrators the latitude to respond in accordance with the unique characteristics of each student and situation. Principals need the authority to employ their professional judgment in concert with the skills of staff members knowledgeable about child development, behavior, mental health, and classroom management.

Parents are an important part of the equation as well. Their understanding of and investment in reasonable discipline policies not only reduces potential liability, but also enhances the effectiveness of discipline practices. Signing a discipline policy is not enough. School leaders need to engage parents in policy development, communication around developmentally appropriate considerations and expectations for students, and ongoing prevention programming.

We all have a stake in ensuring safe, orderly, and civil learning environments. To do that, though, we must stop expecting, and then promoting, sound-bite solutions to complex issues. In conflating the commitment to prevent misbehavior with a mandate for uniformly harsh punishment, we limit our ability to focus on proven practices.

Discipline and punishment are not synonymous, and we need to separate the two. If not, we simply will build more and bigger woodsheds, at a cost measured in wasted public dollars, missed learning opportunities, and, for some, the lost potential of children's lives.

Organizations to Contact

The editors have compiled the following list of organizations concerned with the issues debated in this book. The descriptions are derived from materials provided by the organizations. All have publications or information available for interested readers. The list was compiled on the date of publication of the present volume; the information provided here may change. Be aware that many organizations take several weeks or longer to respond to inquiries, so allow as much time as possible.

American Family Association (AFA)
PO Drawer 2440, Tupelo, MS 38803
(662) 844-5036 • fax: (662) 842-7798
Web site: www.afa.net

Founded in 1977, AFA represents and stands for traditional family values, focusing primarily on the influence of television and other media on society. Though it does not support censorship, AFA advocates responsibility and accountability of the entertainment industry. AFA publishes a monthly newsletter and *AFA Journal*.

American Federation of Teachers (AFT)
555 New Jersey Ave. NW, Washington, DC 20001
(202) 879-4400
Web site: www.aft.org

The AFT was founded in 1916 to represent the economic, social, and professional interests of classroom teachers. It has more than 3,000 local affiliates nationwide, 43 state affiliates, and more than 1.3 million members. It publishes the *PSRP Reporter*, a quarterly newsletter.

Children's Defense Fund (CDF)

25 E Street NW, Washington, DC   20001
(800) CDF-1200 (233-1200)
e-mail: cdfinfo@childrensdefense.org
Web site: www.childrensdefense.org

Founded in 1973, CDF is a nonprofit child advocacy organization that supports policies and programs that aim to lift children out of poverty; protect them from abuse and neglect; and ensure their access to health care, quality education, and a moral and spiritual foundation. The organization publishes "Protect Children, Not Guns," "State of America's Children," and other periodically updated reports.

Justice Policy Institute (JPI)

1003 K Street NW, Suite 500, Washington, DC   20001
(202) 558-7974
e-mail: info@justicepolicy.org
Web site: www.justicepolicy.org

Since 1997, JPI has worked to enhance the public dialogue on incarceration through accessible research, public education, and communications advocacy. Its areas of research and numerous publications and fact sheets cover issues in juvenile justice, delinquency, and gangs, with an emphasis on alternatives to incarceration.

National Institute on Media and the Family

606 24th Ave. South, Suite 606, Minneapolis, MN   55454
(888) 672-KIDS (672-5437) • fax: (612) 672-4113
Web site: www.mediafamily.org

The Institute seeks to educate and inform the public and to encourage practices and policies that promote positive change in the production and use of mass media. It does not advocate censorship of any kind but does aim to partner with parents and other caregivers, organizations, and corporations to create media choices for families.

National Rifle Association (NRA)

11250 Waples Mill Road, Fairfax, VA   22030
(800) 672-3888
Web site: www.nrahq.org

The NRA is a nonprofit organization that seeks to protect the
Second Amendment and other firearms ownership rights in
the United States. It promotes armed self-defense as well as
sponsors firearms safety and marksmanship programs.

National Youth Rights Association (NYRA)

1101 Fifteenth Street NW, Suite 200, Washington, DC   20005
(202) 296-2992 ext. 131
Web site: www.youthrights.org

NYRA is a youth-led national nonprofit organization dedi-
cated to fighting for the civil rights and liberties of young
people. NYRA has members in all 50 states, more than 7,000
in total, and chapters from coast to coast. It seeks to lower the
voting age, lower the drinking age, repeal curfew laws, and
protect student rights.

National School Safety Center (NSSC)

141 Duesenberg Dr., Ste. 11, Westlake Village, CA   91362
(805) 373-9977 • fax: (805) 373-9277
website: www.schoolsafety.us

NSSC serves as an advocate for safe, secure, and peaceful
schools worldwide and as a catalyst for the prevention of
school crime and violence. It provides school communities
and their safety partners with quality information, resources,
consultation, and training services. The center's publications
include *School Discipline Notebook* and *Student Searches and
the Law.*

Office of Juvenile Justice and Delinquency Prevention (OJJDP)

U.S. Department of Justice, Washington, DC   20531
(202) 307-5911
Web site: http://ojjdp.ncjrs.org

OJJDP provides national leadership and resources to prevent and respond to juvenile delinquency. It supports community efforts to develop effective programs and improve the juvenile justice system. Publications available at its Web site include "Domestic Assaults by Juvenile Offenders," "The Girls Study Group—Charting the Way to Delinquency Prevention for Girls," and "Juvenile Transfer Laws: An Effective Deterrent to Delinquency?"

Youth Crime Watch of America (YCWA)

9200 South Dadeland Blvd., Suite 417, Miami, FL   33156
(305) 670-2409 • fax: (305) 670-3805
Web site: www.ycwa.org

YCWA is a nonprofit, student-led organization that promotes crime and drug prevention programs in communities and schools throughout the United States. Member students at the elementary and secondary levels help raise others' awareness concerning youth issues and the importance of education. Strategies include organizing student assemblies and patrols, conducting workshops, and challenging students to become personally involved in preventing crime and violence.

Bibliography

Books

David Cullen   *Columbine.* New York: Hachette Book Group, 2009.

James Garbarino   *See Jane Hit: Why Girls Are Growing More Violent and What We Can Do About It.* New York: Penguin Books, 2006.

Tom Hayden   *Street Wars: Gangs and the Future of Violence.* New York: New Press, 2006.

Gerard Jones   *Killing Monsters: Why Children Need Fantasy, Super Heroes, and Make-believe Violence.* New York, Basic Books, 2003.

Peter Langman   *Why Kids Kill: Inside the Minds of School Shooters.* New York: Palgrave Macmillan, 2009.

Katherine S. Newman, Cybelle Fox, Wendy Roth, Jal Mehta, and David Harding   *Rampage: The Social Roots of School Shootings.* New York: Basic Books, 2005.

Deborah Prothrow-Stith   *Sugar and Spice and No Longer Nice: How We Can Stop Girls' Violence.* San Francisco, CA: Jossey-Bass, 2005.

Howard R. Spivak, Karen Sternheimer   *It's Not the Media: The Truth About Pop Culture's Influence on Children.* Boulder, CO: Westview Press, 2003.

Periodicals

Rodney Balko "Zero Tolerance Makes Zero Sense," *Washington Post*, August 9, 2005.

Christian Science Monitor "Time to Tame TV Violence," May 10, 2007.

Community Care "Impact of Domestic Violence on Children," July 10, 2008.

Julia Dahl "She Killed Her Mom," *Seventeen*, January 2006.

Theodore Dalrymple "Moral Panic Is the Right Reaction," *Spectator*, September 1, 2007.

Kim Fries and Todd A. DeMitchell "Zero Tolerance and the Paradox of Fairness: Viewpoints From the Classroom," *Journal of Law and Education*, April 2007.

Harvard Reviews of Health News "Limiting Kids' Exposures to Violence, Guns," July 11, 2008.

Peter Katel "Fighting Crime: Do Street Gangs Represent a Growing National Problem?" *CQ Researcher*, February 2008.

Melissa Klein "Gang Grief: Violence Wounds Teens and Communities," *Current Health 2*, March 2009.

Marc Lacey "In Mexico, Curbing Violence Before It Is Learned," *New York Times*, January 10, 2009.

Mike Males   "Why Are We So Eager to Fear
                     Youths?" *Perspectives on Youth*,
                     Summer/Fall 2005.

Jennifer Mertens   "Kids With Guns: How Agencies
                     Have Made Strides to Get Guns Out
                     of the Hands of Juveniles," *Law
                     Enforcement Technology*, October
                     2006.

Mark Steyn   "Teenage Wasteland: The
                     Consequences of Extending Our
                     Adolescence at the Expense of
                     Growing Up Are Only Too
                     Predictable," *Western Standard*, July
                     30, 2007.

USA Today   "Cities Grapple With Crime By Kids,"
                     July 12, 2006.

Claudia Wallis   "Does Kindergarten Need Cops?"
                     Time, December 7, 2003.

Nancy Willard   "We Hate Ashley: Counteracting
                     Cyberbullying Inside—and
                     Outside—School Grounds," *District
                     Administration*, September 2008.

Index